How to Set Up Your New Computer

Other Computer Tiles

by

R. A. Penfold

How to Set Up Your New Computer

R. A. Penfold

Bernard Babani (publishing) Ltd
The Grampians
Shepherds Bush Road
London W6 7NF
England
www.babanibooks.com

Please note

Although every care has been taken with the production of this book to ensure that any projects, designs, modifications, and/or programs, etc., contained herewith, operate in a correct and safe manner and also that any components specified are normally available in Great Britain, the Publisher and Author do not accept responsibility in any way for the failure (including fault in design) of any projects, design, modification, or program to work correctly or to cause damage to any equipment that it may be connected to or used in conjunction with, or in respect of any other damage or injury that may be caused, nor do the Publishers accept responsibility in any way for the failure to obtain specified components.

Notice is also given that if any equipment that is still under warranty is modified in any way or used or connected with home-built equipment then that warranty may be void.

© 2005 BERNARD BABANI (publishing) LTD

First Published - July 2005

British Library Cataloguing in Publication Data
A catalogue record for this book is available from the British Library

ISBN   0 85934 559 9

Cover Design by Gregor Arthur
Printed and bound in Great Britain by Cox & Wyman

Preface

A modern PC is a powerful piece of equipment that, with the aid of suitable software and peripheral equipment, can handle a wide range of tasks. By any standards, a PC is a very complex piece of equipment. Matters are further complicated in a real-world PC system, by the array of additional equipment that usually connects to the PC itself. Setting up a new PC and getting it fully operational is not a task that PC experts take lightly. Even if you have years of experience at setting up and using PCs, it can be difficult to iron out the minor difficulties that tend to occur. For those getting their first PC the task is probably quite daunting.

The first job is to get everything connected together properly. A modern PC bristles with sockets, and there are usually plenty of peripheral gadgets to connect to them. Chapter 1 of this book shows you what goes where, how to deal with awkward connectors, and how to get everything plugged together with a minimum of fuss. Many PCs are supplied as complete systems, with peripheral gadgets such as printers and scanners, or these are soon added to the basic system. Chapter 2 covers common problems with popular peripherals such as printers, scanners, and cameras.

The world of computing is not static. Although the rate of change is probably less hectic than it was a few years ago, things still move on at a fast pace. Your newly installed PC system could already be slightly out of date. Chapter 3 deals with obtaining and installing updates or upgrades. This includes updates for Windows, application programs, and the driver software that integrates the computer's hardware with Windows. Getting Windows operating properly and set up to suit your needs is covered in Chapter 4. Finally, Chapter 5 deals with file related problems, including the downloading of plug-ins for Internet Explorer. Everything you need to know in order to get your PC "up and running".

Robert Penfold

Contents

1

2

Peripheral problems 81

3

Updating and fixing 117

4

Windows problems 185

5

Solving file difficulties 235

Terminology

Pointer
This is the onscreen arrow that you move with the mouse. It is not always an arrow, and it changes to an hourglass when the computer is busy.

Cursor
The pointer usually changes to a vertical line when placed over text. It is then the cursor rather then the pointer.

Window
You can have more than one program running at once, with each one operating in its own area of the screen. Each of these areas is a window, and windows are also used for other things such as warning messages and to display graphics.

Left-click
Press and release the left mouse button once.

Double-click
Press and release the left mouse button twice in rapid succession.

Right-click
Press and release the right mouse button.

Drag
Position the onscreen pointer, hold down the left mouse button, move the pointer, and release the left mouse button. Dragging is used to select blocks of text, move onscreen objects, and similar functions.

Icon
An icon is a small onscreen graphic that is used to represent something. The "something" is usually a program, document, or piece of hardware.

Trademarks

Getting it together

Don't panic

Traditionally, PCs are supplied in one large box, but on opening that box you find it contains at least three more boxes. This is due to the fact that a conventional PC is a three unit system that consists of a keyboard, the base unit (the computer itself), and a monitor. With a modern PC there is a fourth unit, which is the mouse (Figure 1.1), but this is often packed in the same box as the keyboard.

Unless you buy a PC that it primarily intended for business use, it is almost certain to be supplied with an amplifier and loudspeakers, but the amplifier is usually built into one of the loudspeakers. There will be at least two speaker units, but there could be six or more!

Modern PCs are often marketed as large systems that contain various peripherals that would once have been very expensive optional extras. These usually offer good value for money and make it relatively easy for a complete beginner to buy and set up a computer system. However, avoid buying systems that contain expensive items that you are unlikely to find useful.

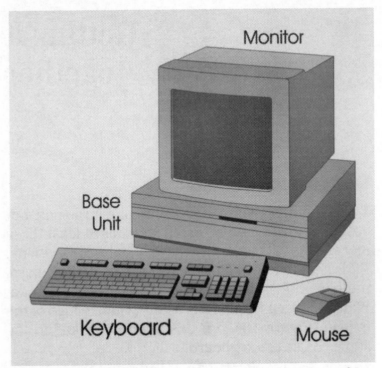

*Fig.1.1 A modern PC consists of three main units
plus a mouse*

An inkjet printer is probably the peripheral that is most frequently bundled with PCs, but digital cameras and scanners are often included as well. The so-called "all-in-one" units are also popular as bundled items. These act as a printer, scanner, and photocopier, and sometimes have a fax facility as well. There could be other units such as games controllers and a headset.

Even if you buy a fairly basic PC system it is likely to arrive in a fairly large box. If you buy an "all singing,

Fig.1.2 An essential item, with a typical PC system requiring from three to five mains outlets

all dancing" PC with bundled peripheral gadgets, it is likely to arrive in several boxes that will all but fill the average room! Avoid the temptation to panic at this stage. The PC system will take up much less space once everything is set up and it is ready to use. On the other hand, do not underestimate the amount of space required for a comprehensive computer system. There is no point in buying a computer system unless you are able to give it a significant amount of space in one corner of a room.

You should really give some thought to the positioning of the PC beforehand, rather than waiting until it arrives. These days the base unit and monitor are powered from separate mains sockets, and further sockets might be needed for major peripheral devices such as printers and scanners. Ideally the computer system should be positioned close to a mains outlet. A four or six way mains adapter (Figure 1.2) will be needed in order to power everything from a single mains outlet.

It is not a good idea to position the system opposite a window. Although monitors have anti-reflective coatings to reduce reflections from the glass screen, no coating approaches complete effectiveness. With the monitor facing a window it is likely that parts of the screen will be very difficult to read during daylight hours. In fact much of the screen could be impossible to read on bright days.

Also avoid having the PC itself, or any part of the system, close to a radiator or heater. Modern PC systems tend to generate substantial amounts of heat, so they need to be positioned where they will keep reasonably cool. Feeding them with additional heat is asking for trouble. When the system is installed and operational, never cover or in any way hinder the flow of air through any ventilation grilles. Doing so could easily result in costly damage to the equipment and could even be dangerous.

Portable PCs

Where space is strictly limited it is worth considering a small PC of some kind. Small versions of desktop

PCs are available, although the amount of desk space required is not necessarily much less than that of a normal tower style PC. A drawback of most of the smaller desktop PCs is that they usually have less scope for expansion. Of course, these days most PCs are supplied as standard with a range of features that would once have been optional extras. Expansion has therefore become less of an issue, but it is something to bear in mind if you intend to add something exotic such as a video capture card or an upmarket sound system.

It is increasingly common for home users to opt for a laptop or notebook PC, even though portability is not an issue. The big advantage of a portable PC is that it can be packed away into a drawer or cupboard when it is not is use. This makes it relatively easy to find somewhere to do your computing. Although portable PCs used to be very high in price and low in specification, the modern units genuinely rival desktop PCs in terms of performance.

There is still additional cost involved with a laptop or notebook PC, but in absolute terms they are not particularly expensive. The lower power consumption of a portable computer gives slightly lower running costs, so it is likely that the additional cost at purchase will be repaid over a period of a few years.

Portable PCs do have a few drawbacks that must be taken into account. As pointed out previously, small desktop PCs have relatively limited potential for expansion. If anything, this problem is even greater with portable PCs. They are simply not designed to be used as the basis of a huge computer system, and trying to use one in this way is probably not a sensible course of action.

This is not to say that portable PCs have no expansion potential. They are usually equipped with high speed USB ports that can be connected to printers, scanners, and digital cameras. In fact a huge range of USB add-ons are available these days, including things like television adapters and advanced audio systems. Consequently, using a portable PC in a specialised application is often quite straightforward, but it is probably best not to get carried away and start connecting all-manner of gadgets to one. Portable PCs are at their best in reasonably simple and straightforward systems.

Another point to bear in mind is that most home PCs are not used in complete isolation. At the very least, you will probably need to use a printer or a multifunction gadget with your PC, and devices such as these require significant amounts of space. It is still worthwhile considering a portable PC if the available space is limited, since being able to pack the PC away still frees space for other purposes. If you start adding further peripherals such as scanners and sets of loudspeakers, the space required by the PC itself will be the least of your problems. Portable PCs are great for home use if you take the "keep it simple" approach, but they are otherwise unlikely to be a good choice.

Getting it together   1

Unpack carefully

When you first receive any new gadget there is a temptation to rush in and get it unpacked and operational as quickly as possible. With something as complex as a PC this is definitely not a good idea. It needs to be unpacked and set up carefully. Unpacking the PC itself is unlikely to pose many problems, but there are sometimes bits of cardboard that have to be carefully removed from the externally accessible disc drives before they can be used. The screen of the monitor might be covered by a translucent plastic sheet that has to be removed before it is used.

The system should be supplied with an instruction manual that gives details of any obscure bits of packing that must be located and removed. These days most computer equipment is supplied complete with a "Getting Started" or "Quick Start" guide that includes information of this type. Always have at least a quick read through with any documentation of this type. It can avoid unnecessary problems later on.

If the system includes a printer or scanner it is virtually certain that these will have some odd bits of packing material that must be removed before trying to use the equipment. Scanners and printers have moving parts that are usually locked in place during transit. They are usually held in place by bits of cardboard, plastic, foam material, and the like. These are often hidden somewhere inside the equipment. Some units, and scanners in particular, have a proper locking mechanism that must be released prior to use (Figure 1.3).

It is very important to carefully read the documentation supplied with the system, and to remove any bits of concealed packing material, undo

any locking mechanisms, or whatever. An attempt to use the equipment without doing so is likely to result in problems such as chewed-up bits of packing material getting into the mechanism, a fuse "blowing", etc. The

Fig.1.3 As supplied, the head of a scanner is often locked

equipment could easily become damaged, and the guarantee is unlikely to cover this type of thing.

Getting connected

Once everything has been unpacked it is time to start connecting everything together. Unfortunately, computer systems usually have quite a number of cables to connect, which can make things a bit confusing at first. Probably the best place to start is with the mouse and keyboard. There is a port

*Fig.1.4 A PS/2 connector (left) and the original
type of keyboard connector (right)*

specifically for a mouse, but some mice are instead
designed for use with a USB (universal serial bus)
port. A USB port is a general-purpose type that can
be used with a wide variety of peripherals, and most
modern PCs have several of them. A keyboard also
has its own special port, but once again, some are
designed for use with a USB port.

It is easy to tell which type of mouse or keyboard you
have, since the standard keyboard/mouse connector
looks very different to a USB type. The original PC
keyboard connector was a large 5-way DIN plug, as
on the right in Figure 1.4. This type of connector is
intended for use in audio equipment, but it did the job
perfectly well. It has now been replaced by a

miniature version, as shown on the left in Figure 1.4, and you will only obtain the old type if you buy a pretty old second-hand PC. The new type of connector is usually called a PS/2 type, as it was first used on IBM's PS/2 range of PCs.

Mouse

The original mice connected to a serial port of the PC, or to a port provided by a special expansion card. Both of these methods are obsolete and have not been used on new PCs for a number of years. Modern PCs have a port specifically designed for use with a mouse. Rather unhelpfully perhaps, the mice that are used with this port also have a PS/2 connector. Consequently, there is nothing to prevent users from getting the mouse plugged into the keyboard port and the keyboard connected to the mouse port.

Getting the mouse and keyboard connections swapped over is unlikely to cause any problems, but it is best not to put this type of thing to the "acid test". Modern PCs, keyboards, and mice have the connectors colour coded in order to make it obvious which device connects to each of the sockets. In fact a number of the connectors used on modern PCs have this colour coding in an attempt to avoid confusion and errors when installing a new computer system.

In the case of the mouse and keyboard, they are respectively a light green colour and mauve. Consequently, there should be no real danger of getting them swapped over. Just fit the plugs into

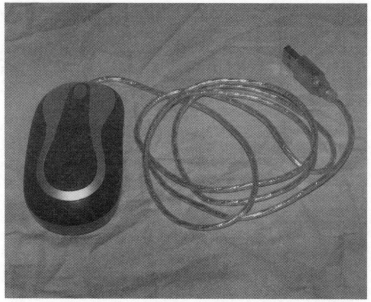

*Fig.1.5 These days many mice connect to a USB
port rather than the PS/2 mouse port*

the sockets of the same colour and everything should
be fine.

USB mouse

These days it is quite common for new PCs to be
supplied with a mouse that connects to a USB port
rather than the mouse port. A typical USB mouse is
shown in Figure 1.5, and a close-up of the USB plug is
shown in Figure 1.6. The keyboard might also be a
USB type.

USB stands for universal serial bus, and as the name
implies, it is a general-purpose port that can be used

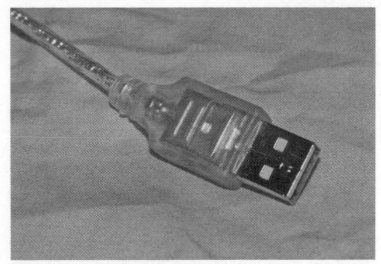

Fig.1.6 The flat shape of a USB plug is not like any other type of connector used with a PC

for practically any peripheral gadget. Most PCs have several USB ports, and there are USB hubs that can be used to provide even more from one of the existing USB ports. When it was first introduced, USB was intended to be the new way of connecting just about any type of peripheral device to a PC. To a large extent it has fulfilled this design aim.

You need to be aware that some keyboards and mice are of the so-called "wireless" variety. Normally the mouse and keyboard are powered from the PC, but this is clearly not possible if there is no connecting cable from the PC to the keyboard or mouse. Wireless peripherals are usually powered by one or two AA or AAA cells. A set of batteries should really be included with the system, but in practice this will not necessarily be the case.

The connection from the computer to the keyboard or mouse is provided by an infrared or radio link. Both methods require a receiver that is connected to the appropriate port or ports of the PC via a short cable. Some receivers connect to a USB port while others connect to one or both of the PS/2 ports. A connection diagram should be supplied with the equipment, but it should be possible to determine which type of port is used by looking at to see what type of plug is used on the receiver.

Which USB port?

In general, it does not matter which USB port is used for a given peripheral, since all the USB ports of a PC are identical. There are actually two types of USB port, which are the original (USB 1.1) and the new high-speed version (USB 2.0), but it is very unlikely that your PC will have a mixture of the two.

Unless you buy a second-hand PC it will certainly have USB 2.0 ports. These can be used with any USB devices, including USB 1.1 types. Of course, things work at the old USB 1.1 speed if you use a slow peripheral with a high-speed USB port. With anything like this the system is always limited to the speed of the slowest part of the system.

If you are using an older PC that has USB 1.1 ports, it will work with most USB 2.0 devices, but some will not operate at all without the additional speed of a

Fig.1.7 The port cluster on the rear of a PC

USB 2.0 port. Other units will work with an old USB port, but more slowly and not necessarily in a worthwhile fashion. Neither a keyboard nor a mouse requires high-speed operation, so both should work perfectly well with any USB port.

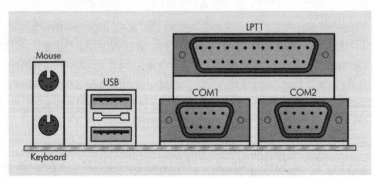

Fig.1.8 The labels identify the ports in the
photograph of Figure 1.7

Finding the ports

Modern PCs are not exactly short of ports, with a number of then on the rear panel. Often there is a further selection on the front panel, although these are often concealed behind a sliding or hinged panel. The mouse and keyboard ports are normally in the main cluster on the rear of the base unit. With a PC that has some form of tower (vertical) case, the cluster of ports is positioned near the top and on the left-hand side (as viewed from the rear). With a desktop (horizontal) case, it is near the bottom and well towards the left end of the case (again, as viewed from the rear). It should not be difficult to find.

A typical port cluster is shown in Figure 1.7, and Figure 1.8 identifies the ports in a typical cluster. These days it is probably a mistake to talk in terms of a typical cluster. The number of ports included in the standard specification has increased over the years, rendering the usual arrangements inadequate for many PCs. The ports shown in Figure 1.7 represent the minimum complement for a modern PC.

Particularly with the more upmarket PCs, there will probably be more ports than shown in Figure 1.7. Most of the standard ports will be in there somewhere, but you might have to do a little searching. Some of the older ports are being phased out, but this is unlikely to be of any importance for anyone buying their first PC. Figure 1.9 shows the port cluster of a PC motherboard that was selected at random, and these are the ports that it provides:

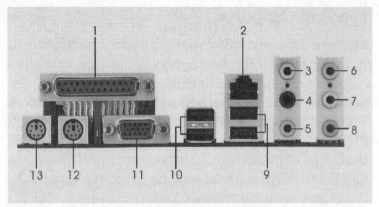

*Fig.1.9 A modern PC often has a large number of
ports in the main cluster on the rear panel*

1   Parallel Port

2   RJ-45 (networking) Port

3   Side Speaker

4   Rear Speaker

5   Central/Bass Speaker

6   Line In

7   Front Speaker

8   Microphone

9   USB 2.0 Ports

10 USB 2.0 Ports

11 VGA (monitor) Port

12 PS/2 Keyboard Port

13 PS/2 Mouse Port

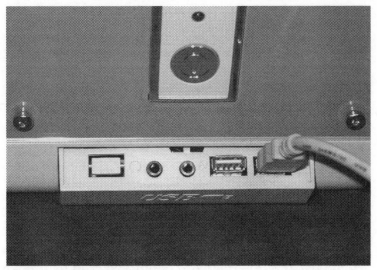

*Fig.1.10   There might be some ports on the PC's
        front panel*

Their flat shape make USB connectors sufficiently
different to other types of computer connector for
there to be little difficulty in locating the
corresponding sockets on the rear of the PC. There
should be as least two of them, but there could well
be four or even six USB ports. As pointed out
previously, modern PCs often have some sockets on
the front panel. These are often concealed behind a
panel, or are on a drop-down panel, so you might have
to do some searching in order to reveal them. The
drop-down panel shown in Figure 1.10 has two audio
sockets on the left and two USB ports on the right.

There are two reasons for having connectors at the
front of the unit. One is to make it easy to access

sockets that will be needed quite often. The other is simply that some devices are used in front of the PC, so it makes sense to have the corresponding connectors at the front of the base unit. The mouse and keyboard are used in front of the base unit, so I suppose that having sockets for them at the front of the PC is logical. In practice it is far from common to have front-mounted PS/2 mouse and keyboard sockets.

The situation is different with USB ports. If a PC has some front-mounted sockets, it is virtually certain that at least two of them will be USB sockets. Whether or not it is a good idea to use these sockets for a USB keyboard and (or) mouse is debatable, and I suppose it is really just a matter of personal preference. Leads sticking out the front of a PC can tend to get in the way, and get tangled up with things on the worktop. My preference is to connect them to the rear of the PC. This leaves the USB ports at the front free for use with small gadgets such as card readers and digital cameras.

Fitting

"It does not fit" is a common complaint when newcomers to the world of computing try to connect everything together. The computer manufacturers' help lines apparently receive numerous calls from the owners of new PCs who can not get one item or another connected to the base unit. An important point to bear in mind is that the orientation of plugs

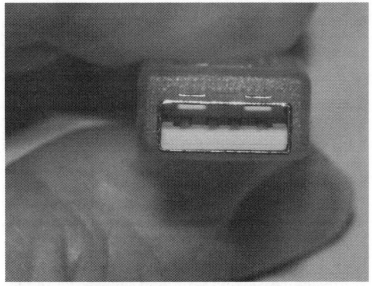

*Fig.1.11 A USB plug has one half solid and the
        other half hollow*

is often important. There are exceptions, such as the
miniature jack plugs that are often used in computer
audio systems, but in most cases a plug will not fit if it
is upside-down, or even if it is rotated a few degrees
from the correct orientation.

The correct orientation often becomes obvious if you
look carefully at both connectors. This is not always
the case though, and it is often difficult to get a really
good look at the connectors tucked away at the back
of a PC. If you look at a USB plug you will see that it
has one half solid and the other half hollow (Figure
1.11). The connector on the PC has a complementary
arrangement that makes it impossible to fit the plug
upside-down (Figure 1.12).

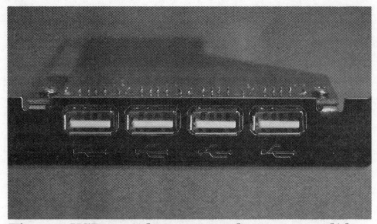

*Fig.1.12 USB ports have a complementary solid
and hollow arrangement*

If it is not possible to see the connector on the PC
properly, just try the plug one way, and if that fails,
try the opposite orientation. The "hammer and tongs"
approach is not the right one with electronic
equipment, and attempting to force plugs into sockets
is likely to damage something. A plug will fit into a
socket once the orientation is correct.

It will not fit into a socket properly if the orientation
is not correct, and shoving a bit harder will not change
that fact. It might damage one of the connectors
though, and this type of thing is unlikely to be covered
by the guarantee. New connectors are notorious for
being a bit reluctant to fit together, but some wiggling
and no more than firm pressure is more likely to be
successful than using brute force.

PS/2 connectors are more difficult than the USB
variety since their orientation has to be correct within

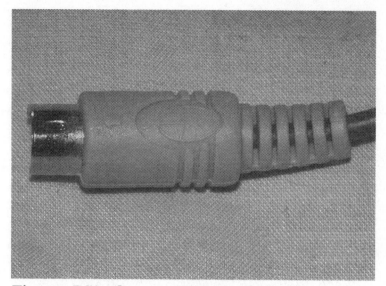

Fig.1.13 PS/2 plugs are often marked with an arrow

a few degrees before they will fit into place. If you look at a PS/2 plug it will either have an arrow moulded into the casing (Figure 1.13), or one side of the casing will be flat (Figure 1.14). With a desktop case the arrow or the flat side of the casing faces upwards. A tower case is effectively a desktop type resting on one side. When looking at the sockets on the rear of a tower case, the arrow or flat side of the connector's casing should be on the right.

With the orientation correct, PS/2 and similar plugs will usually fit into the sockets without any difficulty. Once again, if the plug will not fit, even after some judicious wiggling, do not try to force it into place. Look at the plug to see if any of the pins are bent.

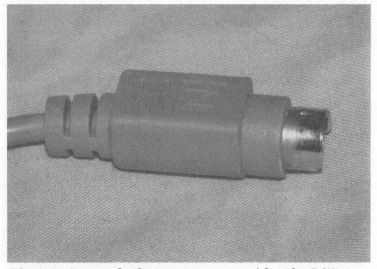

*Fig.1.14 Instead of an arrow, one side of a PS/2
plug might be flat*

Even one pin bent slightly out of position can be
sufficient to prevent a miniature plug from being fitted
into place. The problem can usually be cured by
gently prising the offending pin back into position
using the blade of a small screwdriver. The pins of a
usable plug look like the ones shown in Figure 1.15.

Video

The cluster of ports might include an output for the
monitor. This is likely to be the case with a PC
intended for business use or with a budget type. With
both of these types it is quite normal for the video
circuits to be included on the motherboard.
Integrated graphics are not used with PCs that are

Fig.1.15 The pins of a PS/2 plug should look like this

designed to have fast 3D capability, such as a computer intended for games use.

Instead, computers of this type have the graphics on a special expansion card, and the socket for the monitor is on this card. It is still situated on the rear of the computer, but away from the main cluster of connectors (Figure 1.16).

The original PC video connector was a 9-pin D type, but this was superseded by a 15-pin D type some years ago. This connector is still in use with modern analogue monitors, which includes all units that have a CRT (cathode ray tube). In other words, it includes all monitors of the traditional (large) type. The situation is less clear-cut with the various types of flat-

Fig.1.16 The standard analogue video connector for PCs is a 15-way D type

panel monitors such as the LCD type. Some of these are only equipped with a 15-pin D connector, but others also have a new type of video connector for a digital signal.

On the rear of the computer there should be a 15-pin D connector, but a digital output is far from universal. Where both the monitor and the PC support a digital connection, the best results should be obtained by using this method of connection. There is clearly no choice in situations where one or both units lack support for digital operation, and an analogue connection has to be used.

D connectors

Not for nothing are D connectors called D connectors. They are (sort of) D shaped (Figure 1.17), and this ensures that they can not be fitted upside-down. The correct orientation should be self-evident if you look at the two connectors. The connectors can be locked together using two screws on the male connector (the one on the monitor's lead). With modern D connectors the screws have plastic knobs (Figure 1.18) so that they can be tightened using your fingers, and there is no need to use a screwdriver or other tool.

It is not essential to use the locking screws, and this type of connector will fit together quite well without using them. However, computer leads are often quite thick, and monitor leads rate as one of the thickest and heaviest of computer cables.

Fig.1.17 D connectors are (sort of) D shaped

Unless the locking screws are used, moving the base unit or the monitor even slightly is likely to result in the connector coming adrift.

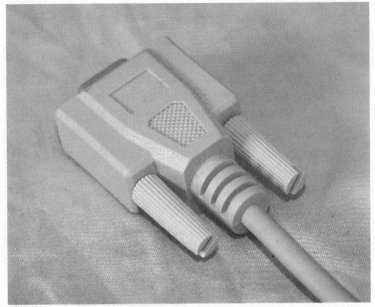

*Fig.1.18 The locking screws of a D plug can be
tightened using your fingers*

Using the locking screws also makes sure that the
connectors fit together reliably. If the locking screws
are not used, it is quite common for the connectors to
fit together at an angle, which prevents proper
electrical contacts from being made. This is
especially problematic when using thick and inflexible
cables that inevitably tend to pull the connectors to
one side or the other. If the locking screws are
adjusted fully into position, the connector should also
be fully in place, and it should stay that way.

Note that most monitors have a captive cable. In
other words, the cable is permanently connected at

*Fig.1.19 The video input socket of a monitor uses
the same connector as a video output*

the monitor end, and it is only necessary to connect it
to the PC's video output. Some of the more expensive
monitors have a D connector on the monitor that is
the same as the one on the PC (Figure 1.19), and are
supplied with a cable that has a male D connector at
each end. This type of cable is connected to the
monitor in exactly the same way as it is connected to
the video output of the PC. The cable can be used
either way round.

Digital

A digital video output uses a connector that looks
much an analogue type at first glance, since it is also
a small D type connector. On closer examination it is

*Fig.1.20 DVI uses a rather more complex version
of a D connector*

clearly different though, so there is little risk of
mistaking one for the other. It is not possible to fit a
digital video plug into an analogue video socket, or
an analogue video plug into a digital video socket, so
there is no risk of using the wrong video output.

Matters are complicated by the fact that there is now
a connector that is used to provide both analogue and
digital video signals (Figure 1.20). This is known as
DVI (digital video interface), and it is used for other
types of video equipment. Who knows, there could
be further developments by the time you read this,
but DVI is gaining in popularity and will probably
become the new standard for monitors.

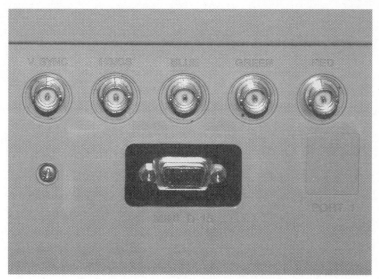

Fig.1.21 Some monitors have five BNC sockets in addition to the usual D type

Fortunately, things should be relatively straightforward for the new PC buyer. The manufacturer of the PC should ensure that the video output or outputs of the PC matches the input or inputs of the monitor. The system should be supplied with a cable that will provide the best form of connection between the two.

BNC

Some monitors and video cards have a set of five connectors, known as BNC connectors, to carry the video signal. You might find that your monitor has these sockets (Figure 1.21), but even on the more upmarket monitors they are now becoming something of a rarity. Few video adapters that use BNC sockets were ever made, and they are pretty rare these days. BNC leads are fairly easy to fit and lock into position, and the connectors utilise a simple bayonet mechanism. The five leads carry the red, green, and blue, signals, plus separate horizontal and vertical synchronisation signals.

Clearly, you have to be very careful not to get any of the connections swapped over. The sockets should be clearly marked with their functions, although usually in abbreviated form (R, G, B, H, and V). This is probably all academic though, and it is very unlikely that you will use a computer system that uses this method of connection. If your monitor has BNC connectors it will almost certainly have a standard 15-way D connector as well, and it is this that will be used to connect it to the PC.

New PC users sometimes get worried about connectors on the PC that do not connect to anything. Quite reasonably, they are concerned because connectors would surely not be put there by the manufacturer unless they were supposed to connect to something. However, PCs, and the components used in them, are often designed to operate with a variety of equipment. They are often designed to operate with old and new equipment, expensive and basic equipment, and varying degrees of the two.

Another point to bear in mind is that PCs are designed to operate with an array of peripheral gadgets, but few people actually use anything approaching the full

Fig.1.22 Serial ports are being phased out

range of available add-ons. Accordingly, there will
often be connectors that are left unused. In the case
of a monitor that has 15-pin D and BNC connectors,
only one or the other will be used. At least one
connector will therefore be left unused, but the system
will still work perfectly well.

Legacy ports

The main cluster of ports at the rear of a PC usually
includes some of the so-called legacy ports. These
are ports that were once used as the main means for
a PC to communicate with peripheral gadgets such
as modems and printers. However, these days there
are more modern ports available for this type of thing,
such as the USB and Firewire types. Consequently,

these older ports are now little used and will ultimately be phased out altogether.

I have yet to see a PC that does not include at least one or two legacy ports as part of its standard specification, but computers that totally lack these ports will probably be the norm before too long. Serial ports, which are also known as RS232C ports, certainly seem to be in decline. Every PC used to have two of these ports as standard, but many now have just the one. A few lack any serial ports as standard, although the computer usually contains the necessary electronics. An optional bracket and lead is all that is normally needed in order to add a pair of serial ports to the rear of the PC.

The original PC serial ports used 25-way D connectors, which was the standard type for an RS232C type. Later PCs used a simplified arrangement and 9-way D connectors. If your PC has serial ports, they will be provided by 9-pin male D connectors. These look a bit like the 15-way analogue video connectors, and are exactly the same size and shape. However, on close inspection they are clearly a bit different, with fewer pins (Figure 1.22).

Are serial ports of any importance in modern computing? Many computer users have old peripherals that are still working well and would be quite expensive to replace. For them, it is important for a PC to have a serial port or two, since they would like to delay replacing their expensive serial port

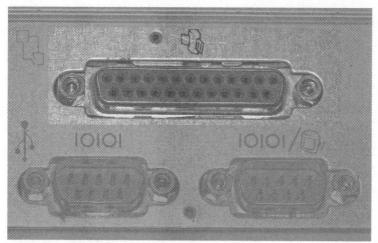

Fig.1.23 The once essential parallel port is also in decline

peripherals for as long as possible. For new users the situation is very different. They lack any legacy devices to connect to the legacy ports, and it is unlikely that they will ever buy any.

Legacy or obsolete?

Buying a device that requires a legacy port, even if it is on offer at an attractive price, is probably not a good idea. With a new PC it is best to buy new and up-to-date gadgets to go with it. Even if your PC has the right type of port to connect to a peripheral, it can still be difficult or impossible to get old devices to work properly with new PCs. Practically all peripheral devices require driver programs to be installed on the PC to enable them to work with the Windows operating system. It is often impossible to obtain

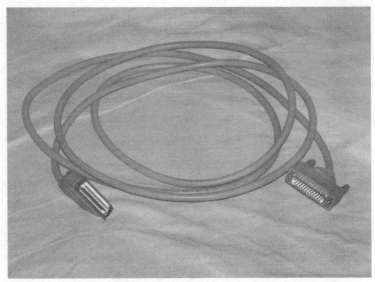

Fig.1.24 A parallel printer lead is still an "off the shelf" item that should be trouble-free

driver software to enable old gadgets to operate with modern versions of Windows.

Another point to keep in mind is that serial ports are notoriously difficult to use. The serial ports at both ends of the link have to be set for the same baud rate (speed), and other parameters also have to be set correctly. Finding a serial cable that will work with your particular PC and peripheral gadget can also be problematic. Getting a serial connection to work exactly as it should tends to be difficult and time consuming even for the experts. Where possible, avoid using the serial ports!

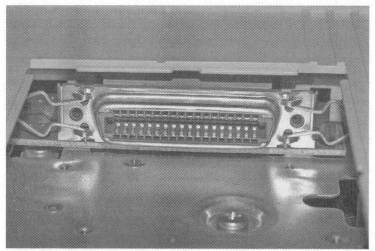

*Fig.1.25 A Centronics parallel port on a laser
        printer*

Printer port

Using the other legacy ports, including the parallel
printer type, is also likely to give problems. The
printer port still seems to be present in the port
clusters of most PCs, and it is the 25-way female D
connector (Figure 1.23). Despite its name, a printer
port can be used with many different types of
peripheral, including such things as external disc
drives and music players. You may encounter
references to "parallel" and "Centronics" ports, which
are just alternative names for the printer port.

Printer ports are probably used much more than the
serial variety, but for new computer users it is still
advisable to avoid using them as far as reasonably

possible. In the early days of computing there were sometimes problems with printer cables, but the cables and connections have become properly standardised over the years. Any computer shop should be able to supply a parallel printer cable (Figure 1.24) that will provide the right connections from a PC to a printer that has a parallel port.

The parallel port on the printer uses a different connector to the one on the computer (Figure 1.25). A 36-way Centronics connector is used on the printer. Instead of screws to hold the plug in place there are usually a couple of wire loops that clip onto the plug.

Note that it is unusual for parallel port peripherals other than printers to use a printer cable. Scanners, external drives, and most other parallel port peripherals use a cable that has a 25-way D connector at each end. Sometimes the cable used is a standard "off the shelf" type, but some of them are "specials" that are designed for one particular gadget or family of gadgets. Losing or accidentally damaging one of these special cables is definitely not a good idea!

Modern printers connect to the PC via a USB port. At one time it was quite common for printers to have a parallel printer port as well, but few current models include this facility. Similarly, other parallel port add-ons are now only produced in USB versions. If you do not have any legacy devices, it makes sense not to lumber yourself with any.

When you buy most peripheral gadgets they are supplied complete with a cable to connect them to the appropriate port of the PC. However, the convention is for printers to be sold without a connecting cable. This was the way things were done in the days when printers had parallel ports, and it seems to have been carried forward into the USB era. With one or two exceptions, printer manufacturers never supply connecting cables with their printers.

One might reasonably expect that a printer cable would be supplied when a printer is supplied as part of a complete PC system. This is not always the case, and you might find that this cable is an optional extra or that you are expected to supply your own. This type of thing is often an overpriced or grossly overpriced optional extra. Buying a USB printer cable from a local computer store or computer fair is likely to be much cheaper.

Game port

Another legacy port you might encounter is the game type. This uses a 15-way D connector (Figure 1.26), which is essentially a slightly larger version of the 9-way type used for serial ports. The original purpose of a game port was to permit joysticks and similar devices to be used with a PC. A later development turned this port into a combined game and MIDI port. In this context MIDI stands for Musical Instruments Digital Interface.

A MIDI port enables suitably equipped musical instruments to be connected together, connected to a computer or other control device, to be used with

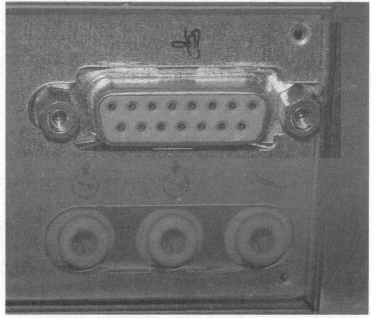

*Fig.1.26 The game port is now obsolete, and it is
unlikely to be present on a new PC*

audio mixers, and so on. This is clearly a rather
specialised type of port that is crucial if you wish to
use a PC with electronic musical instruments, but it
is otherwise of limited use. In fact it is probably of no
use at all outside the sphere of electronic music
production.

It seems likely that the game port will be the first of
the legacy ports to completely "bite the dust". Few
new PCs have this type of port, and it seems likely
that it will be dropped completely in the near future.
Manufacturers of games controllers soon made the

*Fig.1.27 These days most games controllers, like
this one, connect to a USB port*

switch to USB operation when this type of port first
became available.   Using a USB port for a games
controller gave much more scope for adding clever
facilities. It opened up new possibilities that were way
beyond the scope of a game port. Fairly simple USB
games controllers such as the unit shown in Figure
1.27 are often bundled with PCs intended for home
use. If you require something more exotic it usually
has to be purchased separately.

The MIDI capability of a game port was not as good
as it might have been. Merging this facility into an
existing port enforced compromises, and meant that
the PC version of a MIDI port was non-standard. For

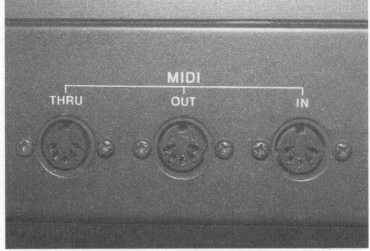

Fig.1.28 A standard set of MIDI ports. These will only be present if the PC has an upmarket sound system

a start, it did not use the right kind of connector. A form of DIN connector originally intended for audio use is the standard type for MIDI systems. Figure 1.28 shows a normal set of MIDI ports.

An adapter containing some simple electronics was needed in order to implement a full set of proper MIDI ports. A simple but difficult to obtain add-on was therefore needed in order to make use of the MIDI facility. Many users ignored the game port and instead fitted a MIDI expansion card or a sound card that had proper MIDI ports.

If your PC should happen to have a game port, ignoring it would seem to be the smart thing to do. There is little point in obtaining gadgets that require a port which is on the verge of extinction, especially when there are much better alternatives available at quite low prices. It is probably time to throw away any existing gadgets that need a game port. They are unlikely to be usable with a new PC.

Audio

Like many other aspects of modern computing, the audio capabilities have grown enormously over the years. The original PCs were fitted with a loudspeaker, but there was no proper hardware to drive it. The purpose of the loudspeaker was to generate simple "beep" sounds. Most modern PCs still have this internal loudspeaker, and it produces a "beep" or two just after the PC has been switched on. This indicates that the built-in test routine has found nothing wrong. If an error occurs, either a different set of "beeps" will be produced, or there will be no sound from the internal loudspeaker.

There were actually some simple programs that enabled the internal loudspeaker to produce music, and one or two pieces of software even produced synthesised speech. Modern computing soon required something much better than this, and various add-on soundcards were produced. The SoundBlaster cards were the most popular in the early days, but other manufacturers produced soundcards.

These days it is the norm for sophisticated audio circuits to be integrated with the main electronics of

Fig.1.29 A typical set of three audio connectors on the rear of a PC

a PC, although soundcards are still used where even greater sophistication is required. Therefore, the audio connectors are usually to be found in the main cluster, but they might be situated elsewhere on the rear of the PC. They are easy to find since they are not like any other type of connector used on a PC. The standard audio connector used on PCs is the 3.5 millimetre jack or stereo jack variety, which is the same type that is normally used for headphones and earphones on Walkmans, etc. Figure 1.29 shows a typical set of three audio connectors on the rear of a PC.

As pointed out previously, modern PCs often have some audio connectors on the front panel, where they

*Fig.1.30 There will often be headphone and
microphone sockets on the front panel*

are easily accessed (Figure 1.30). These are usually
in addition to rather than instead of the audio
connectors on the rear panel. In general, and where
this facility is available, it is better to use the audio
connectors at the front of the PC.

The audio connectors at the rear of a PC are usually
colour coded, although they normally have legends
as well. This colour coding seems to be much less
common for audio connectors at the front of a PC.
This is presumably because the legends or symbols
for the connectors at the front are much easier to see.
The labels for the sockets at the rear of a PC are often
difficult to see properly, so the colour coding is very
helpful. There should be four audio connectors, but

many PCs only have three of them. This is the full set of four:

Function	Colour
Microphone	Pink
Loudspeaker	Orange
Line output	Lime green
Line input	Light blue

Computers that have an advanced audio system will have some or all of these outputs in addition to or instead of those listed above:

Function	Colour
Front loudspeakers	Lime green
Side loudspeakers	Grey
Rear loudspeakers	Black
Central/bass loudspeakers	Orange

These are the PC 99 colour codes for the non-audio ports:

Function	Colour
USB port	Black
PS/2 Mouse port	Green
PS/2 Keyboard port	Purple

Monitor port	Blue
Serial port	Teal/turquoise
Game port	Yellow-orange
Parallel port	Burgundy

Active speakers

PCs are generally used with "active" or "powered" loudspeakers, which are loudspeakers that have a built-in amplifier. Consequently, it is not considered important for a PC to have a built-in amplifier, as it would simply duplicate the electronics in the loudspeakers. Also, modern PCs often have quite high power consumptions, and generate a fair amount of heat. Having a powerful amplifier built into the PC would result in even higher power consumption and more heat for the cooling system to get rid of.

Incidentally, do not worry if you notice a fair amount of noise coming from your new PC when you switch it on. Most PCs now have two or three cooling fans to expel the heat generated by the power supply, microprocessor, video circuits, etc. Manufacturers seem to be taking steps to reduce the noise levels generated by PCs, but many of them are still quite noisy.

Because the loudspeaker output is likely to be superfluous, it is sometimes omitted. This is very often the case where a PC has the audio circuits on the main board rather than provided by an expansion card. The line output is the one that connects to the input of active loudspeakers, and on many PCs it is actually labelled something like "SPKR" or "LS". However, if it is colour coded green, it is only a low-level output that can not directly drive ordinary loudspeakers that lack an integral amplifier.

Where a genuine loudspeaker (orange) output is present, it is unlikely that the maximum output power will be very high, or that the audio quality will be very good. Consequently, most users prefer to use active loudspeakers, most of which can provide quite high volume levels with reasonably good sound quality. Any loudspeakers supplied with the system will almost certainly be of the active variety, and will work best connected to the line output.

Many of the loudspeaker outputs can only provide very limited maximum output powers, and are only intended for use with little high efficiency loudspeakers of the type that are sometimes used with portable audio gadgets. In fact they are probably included more for use with headphones than loudspeakers, and most PC loudspeaker outputs work well with a wide range of headphones.

A line output socket will sometimes give good results with headphones, but the maximum volume that can be attained is often very limited. There can also be an almost total lack of bass. A loudspeaker output is usually a better option where no dedicated headphone output is available, but in some cases you have to be careful to avoid excessive sound levels.

Practically all modern PCs have a line input, but this is unlikely to be used by most users. It enables the output of something like a tape deck or FM tuner to be connected to the computer's sound system. This permits the signal fed to the line input to be played through the computer's loudspeakers, or with suitable software it can be recorded, copied to an audio CD, converted into MP3 files, and so on. Obviously this facility is extremely useful to some PC users, but in practice it is something that few people ever seem to use.

Microphone

Microphone inputs tend to be a bit problematic. One reason for this is simply that there are several types of microphone in common use, and an input that is suitable for one type will not necessarily work properly with other types. Another problem is that the original SoundBlaster microphone input was a mono type that included a supply output to power an old-fashioned carbon microphone (as used in old telephone handsets).

Some modern sound systems still have this type of microphone input, although these days it would be used with a modern electret microphone. Some modern PC sound systems have a stereo microphone input and no supply output. These are suitable for dynamic microphones, or for electret types that have a built-in battery. Finding out which type of microphone will work with a given PC is usually a matter of trying the "suck it and see" method.

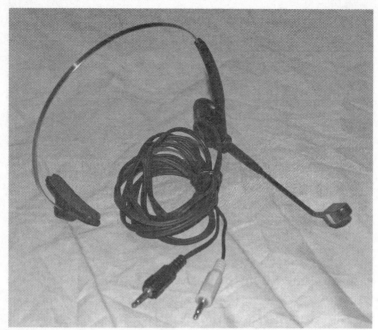

*Fig.1.31 PCs are sometimes supplied complete
with a headset*

Fortunately, this is academic for most PC users.
Unless you wish to use a voice recognition program
or record speech using your PC, it is unlikely that you
will need to bother with a microphone. If you obtain
a voice recognition program it will probably be
supplied complete with a headset that includes a
microphone. With luck, you can just plug this into
the appropriate pair of sockets and it will work.

While it is not exactly a standard item of equipment,
some PCs are supplied with a headset that includes
a microphone. Figure 1.31 shows a headset that is
intended for use with a PC. Many of the microphones

used in these headsets incorporate noise cancelling that is intended to combat general noise in an office, and the noise from the PC.

One can reasonably expect that a headset supplied with a PC will be properly matched to its audio system, and that the microphone will work without any problems. Where the PC has audio sockets at the front, it will probably be better to connect the headset to these rather than using the sockets at the rear of the base unit. The plugs on headsets intended for PC use are often colour coded so that they match the corresponding connectors on the rear of the PC.

Note that some of the more upmarket headsets do not connect to the audio connectors at all. Instead, they connect to the PC via a USB port. Headsets of this type often have some integral digital processing that is intended to give better results with speech recognition programs. Anyway, it will be obvious if the PC is supplied with a headset of this type, since it will be fitted with a USB connector, or it will have an adapter that has a USB connector.

Basic connection

PCs are infamous for the array of cables found in a typical system, and the sound system is likely to add significantly to the normal complement. The wiring of the sound system can be a bit confusing because, once again, there are likely to be one or two sockets that are not used. With a basic (two loudspeaker) stereo system the amplifier is usually a stereo type

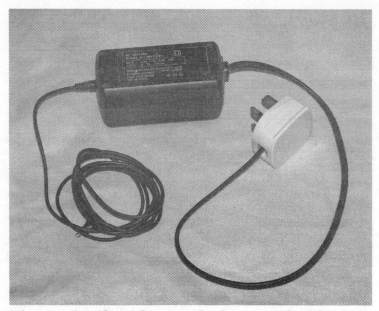

Fig.1.32 Loudspeakers and other peripherals are often powered from a mains adapter

built into one of the loudspeakers. This makes the wiring simpler than the alternative approach of having a mono amplifier in each loudspeaker.

Some active loudspeaker systems are powered direct from the mains, but it is more usual for the lower power types to have a mains adapter (Figure 1.32). This is the method used to power the speaker system used as the basis of this example. The loudspeakers often incorporate shielding which minimises the spread of the magnetic fields generated by the power supply and the loudspeakers themselves. Mains adapters do not normally incorporate any shielding of this type.

The practical importance of this is that it is essential not to have the mains adapter anywhere near the monitor. Conventional monitors that use a cathode ray tube (CRT) are particularly vulnerable to magnetic fields. Placing a mains adapter close to one is more or less guaranteed to produce moving patterns on the picture.

I had one combination of mains adapter and monitor that produced a noticeable degradation of the picture quality if the adapter was brought within about one metre of the monitor. In general, flat panel monitors are far less vulnerable to this type of thing, but it is good practice not to position mains adapters close to any piece of electronics.

Probably the most popular setup is to have the two loudspeakers positioned just to the left and right of the monitor. The magnetic shielding in the loudspeakers prevents them from producing picture interference, but it might still be necessary to have a small gap between each loudspeaker and the monitor.

Some monitors have integral stereo loudspeakers, which makes it much easier to wire up the audio system. You just connect the loudspeaker output or line output of the PC to the audio input of the monitor. Just fit one lead and the audio system is sorted out! The obvious drawback is that you do not have any choice about the positioning of the loudspeakers unless they are detachable.

In the past I have encountered PC audio systems that used phono leads for the interconnections, but these

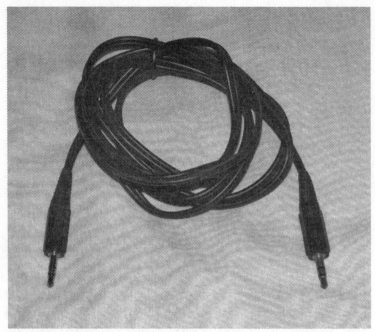

*Fig.1.33 A stereo jack leads carry the connections
from the PC to the main loudspeaker*

days 3.5 millimetre stereo jack leads (Figure 1.33) are
the only type in common use. Even where a mono
signal is being carried, a lead having stereo
connectors is normally used. Sometimes the lead is
a true stereo type but only one half is actually used.
In other cases the connectors are of the stereo variety
but only a mono lead is used to connect them.

This is not purely academic. Where there are two
different types of lead you must use the stereo type
to carry stereo signals and the mono type to carry
mono signals. It will be readily apparent if you get it
wrong, because only one speaker will produce any

*Fig.1.34 The active stereo loudspeaker system
used as the basis of this example*

sound. If there are two types of cable, it is likely that
the mono type will have a normal (round) cable,
whereas the stereo type will have a twin (figure of 8)
cable.

Wiring

The loudspeakers used in this example (Figure 1.34)
are of the usual type that has a stereo amplifier built
into one of the loudspeakers. As is normal practice,

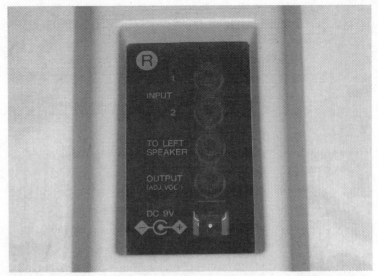

Fig.1.35 The sockets on the rear of the main (right-hand) loudspeaker

the amplifier is in the right-hand loudspeaker, which therefore has the controls such as the on/off switch and volume control. As the system is somewhat lopsided, the sockets at the rear of each loudspeaker are different. The right-hand loudspeaker (Figure 1.35) has a lot more than the left-hand unit (Figure 1.36).

The output of the mains adapter connects to the socket at the bottom. Mains adapters are made with various output voltages and power ratings, and the power plug at the output can have either polarity. This makes it important that the loudspeakers are only used with the adapter that came with them. Do not be tempted to experiment with other units of this type

Fig.1.36 The left-hand loudspeaker only has one socket

that you might happen to have. If there are other gadgets in the computer system that use a mains adapter, make sure that you do not get them swapped over.

Above the power input socket there is an output that is intended for use with an optional subwoofer. Subwoofers are considered in more detail later in this chapter. If it is installed, the sound level from the subwoofer will be controlled via the volume control on the right-hand loudspeaker, as will the sound level from the left-hand loudspeaker. The single socket on the latter connects to the middle socket on the right-hand loudspeaker.

1 Getting it together

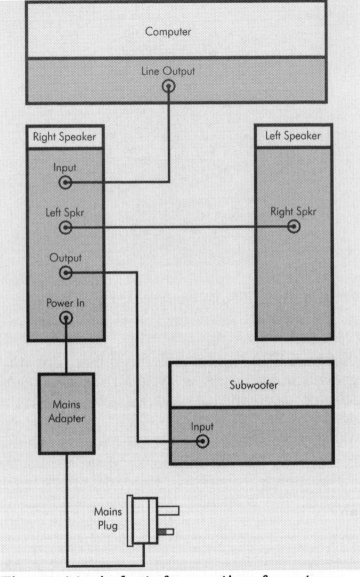

Fig.1.37 A typical set of connections for a stereo sound system with a subwoofer

There are two input sockets at the top, and the loudspeaker output or line output of the PC can be connected to either of these. Two input sockets are provided so that the system can be used with two sources, such as a PC and a personal stereo unit. With some active loudspeaker systems there is a switch that enables one or other of the sources to be selected.

The more common approach, and the one used here, is to have the two inputs feed into a simple mixer circuit. This avoids the need for switching, and whichever source you use will be fed through to the amplifier and loudspeakers. If you use both sources at once, then they will be played simultaneously through the loudspeakers. I suppose this is potentially useful, but is probably of little practical value.

A typical setup with an optional subwoofer would have the interconnections shown in Figure 1.37. The lead from the PC to the right-hand loudspeaker must be a stereo type, but the other audio can be of the mono variety. It is possible that the output for the subwoofer will be a high level type that can drive a passive loudspeaker. However, it is more likely that it will be a low level signal that will require the subwoofer to be an active type having an integral amplifier. The subwoofer might be powered via a mains adapter, but many of these units have a built-in mains power supply unit.

More loudspeakers

As described so far, the PC's audio system has one output socket that can drive a single pair of loudspeakers for normal stereo operation. This is not necessarily what will be supplied with your new PC though. If it is primarily intended for business use it is possible that the PC will not be supplied with loudspeakers at all. Despite this, the PC will almost certainly possess the standard set of audio sockets. This makes it easy to add a pair of loudspeakers, should you need to do so at some future time. There are usually plenty of active loudspeakers to choose from at computer stores and fairs. Some quite good loudspeakers are usually available at surprisingly low prices.

PCs that are intended for home use or specifically aimed at computer gamers are often supplied with about half a dozen loudspeakers. These permit surround sound effects to be produced with the many pieces of games software that supports this feature. The surround sound system supported by most PCs is the Dolby 5.1 type, or a compatible setup.

The "5" in the name indicates that there are five normal speakers, and the ".1" indicates that there is one subwoofer. The latter is a speaker that is specifically designed to reproduce very low frequencies, including those that are too low to be heard. With the volume set high enough, you can feel the vibration from them though. A subwoofer can be

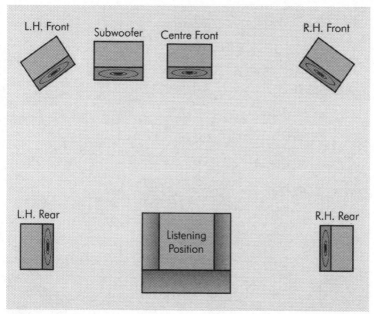

*Fig.1.38 The normal louspeaker positions for a 5.1
surround sound system*

very effective with certain types of game and music.
Some added vibration can give much greater realism
to the explosions in "shoot em up" games for example.

Conventionally, the six speakers are positioned as
shown in Figure 1.38. This is essentially a normal
stereo setup up with the addition of a central speaker
to improve the normal stereo sound stage, and two
rear speakers to give the surround sound effect. It is
difficult to judge the origin of very low frequency
sounds, so the position of the subwoofer is not critical.
The subwoofer is often placed centrally at the rear.

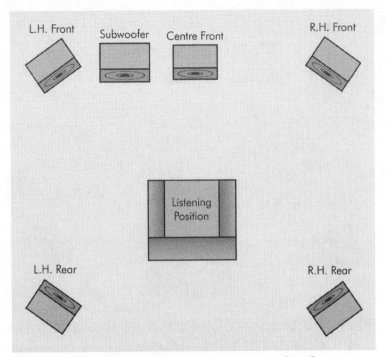

*Fig.1.39 An alternative arrangement for the
loudspeakers in a 5.1 sound system*

Positioning

Opinions tend to differ on the ideal loudspeaker
positioning. Most advocate the user being between
the rear loudspeakers, while others suggest that the
listener should sit further forward (Figure 1.39). The
arrangement of Figure 1.39 is similar to the one that
was used back in the days of four channel hi-fi
systems, but a 5.1 surround sound system is not really
designed for this setup. However, it is really a matter
of personal preference, and how the speakers can

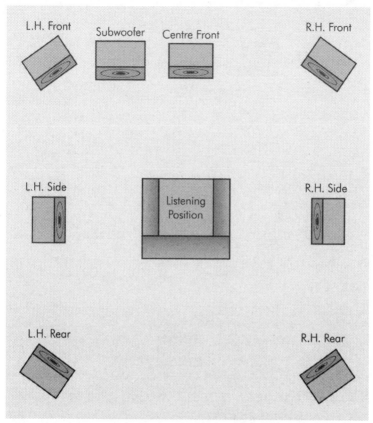

*Fig.1.40 The standard setup used for a 7.1
surround sound system*

reasonably be fitted into the room you are using for
the computer system. With this type of thing it is often
necessary to make compromises due to the
practicalities of the situation.

Note that you can simply use the normal left and right
loudspeakers if you only require normal stereo

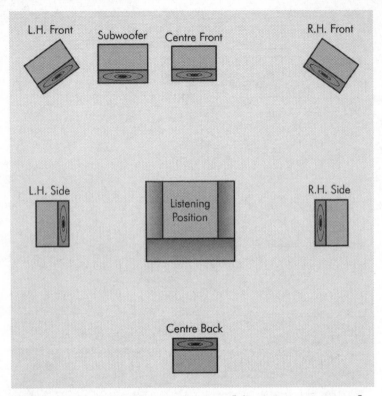

*Fig.1.41 The arrangement used in a 6.1 surround
sound system*

operation. Accommodating six loudspeakers and all
the wiring that goes with them can be difficult, so
there is no point in "going the whole hog" unless you
really require the surround sound effect. Another
point to bear in mind is that the 5.1 system is not the
only type of surround sound used with PCs.

There is also the 4.1 type, which is really just the 5.1
type without the front-centre loudspeaker. There is

also a 7.1 type, which has the 5.1 arrangement plus speakers well to the rear of the listener (Figure 1.40). Although not often encountered in practice, there is a 6.1 system that is a simplified version of the 7.1 type. It has one central loudspeaker at the rear (Figure 1.41) rather than two the two corner units of the 7.1 system.

When connecting the loudspeakers of a surround sound system to a PC it is essential to carefully follow the setting up instructions provided with the PC. There will probably be at least two sets of dedicated loudspeaker outputs (front and rear), but the other loudspeaker outputs might be provided by a line output or one of the other sockets. In other words, one of the sockets might have a dual function, with its role depending on whether the card is being used as a conventional type or a surround sound card. In fact it is possible that more than one socket will have a dual function.

A typical setup for a 5.1 surround sound system is shown in Figure 1.42, and this is basically just an extension of the system used for a stereo sound system. There are three audio outputs on the PC, but each of these carries two channels, The first is for the front stereo channels, the second carries the rear channels, and the third is for the subwoofer and centre-front signals. The three outputs connect to the three inputs on the speaker that contains the amplifier. In this case it is a six-channel amplifier, and there are five loudspeaker outputs. The amplifiers are usually in either the centre-front

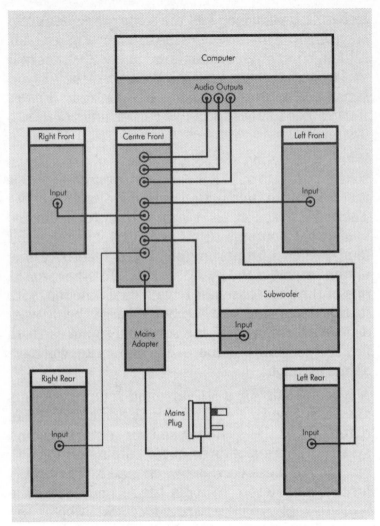

*Fig.1.42 The method of interconnection used in a
        typical 5.1 surround sound system, but
        you might encounter some variations on
        this scheme of things*

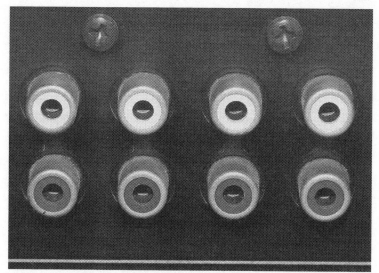

*Fig.1.43 Phono sockets are sometimes used in
surround sound systems*

loudspeaker (as in this example) or the subwoofer.
Each of the other five loudspeakers connects to the
appropriate output of the one that contains the
electronics.

There is clearly much greater scope for making a
mistake when installing a surround sound system.
With a simple stereo setup there is little to get wrong
apart from getting the left and right stereo channels
reversed. This will swap the left and right sides of
the sound stage, but the system will work properly in
other respects and will sound just as good as it would
with normal operation. Getting connections swapped
over with a surround sound system is likely to give
some odd results that do not sound very convincing.

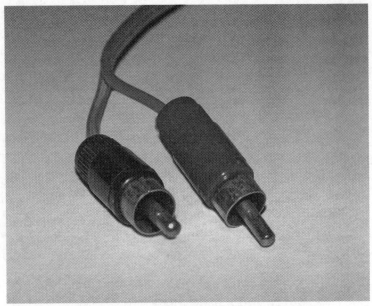

Fig.1.44 There is no stereo version of a phono connector A twin lead is needed

Follow the manufacturer's installation instructions "to the letter", and double-check the connections once you have finished.

With a 5.1 or 7.1 surround sound system it is virtually certain that it will connect to the PC by way of the usual 3.3 millimetre stereo jack leads. The connections from the main speaker to the satellite units are more likely to be carried by phono leads. Phono sockets (Figure 1.43) are a simple 2-way type that can only carry one audio channel. For stereo operation it is necessary to have two sockets and a twin lead with two plugs at each end (Figure 1.44).

However, in this application there is only a single audio signal being carried from the main unit to each satellite loudspeaker, so mono phono leads are used.

The rest

There will sometimes be more ports in the main cluster than those mentioned so far. The most common additional type is an Ethernet port, which is also known as a 10/100 networking port. An Ethernet socket looks very similar to the small telephone sockets used in America and some European countries, but it is actually a different and incompatible type of connector. In Figure 1.45 it is the socket beneath the two PS/2 ports and to the right of the two USB ports.

Ethernet ports are used when connecting several PCs into a network. Networking is a very good idea for small business and home users, since it enables files to be easily moved from one PC to another, and resources such as printers can be shared. However, it requires additional hardware in the form of a router, and it is only applicable if you have at least two PCs. It is not something that is likely to be of use to a first-time PC user.

Firewire is not really a standard PC interface, and it actually has its origins in the world of Macintosh computers. It does feature as standard on some PCs though. Firewire was originally used as a means of connecting a digital video camera or recorder to a computer, and it is still commonly used with digital

Fig.1.45 The Ethernet port is below the PS/2 sockets and to the right of the USB ports

video equipment. It is a high-speed interface that can be used for a wide variety of computer peripherals, so you might need the Firewire ports at some later time. As USB 2.0 is the more popular alternative for PC peripherals, it is more likely that any Firewire ports will not be needed unless you are a digital video enthusiast.

Modem

Most PCs are now supplied with a built-in modem that can be used with a dial-up Internet connection to provide access to the worldwide web. The PC might also be supplied with software that enables the modem to be used for sending and receiving faxes. It is important to realise that a modem of this type is only suitable for a dial-up connection via an ordinary telephone line, and that it can not be used for any form of broadband Internet connection.

The hardware required to implement a broadband connection depends on the particular type you will be using, but it normally requires external hardware that is not supplied as standard with a PC. The broadband supplier will supply details of what you need and how to install it. In many cases the additional hardware is supplied as part of the broadband deal. For a self-install ADSL connection it is usually a USB modem that is supplied, but for some types of broadband connection an Ethernet port is required.

In order to use a built-in modem its Line socket (Figure 1.46) must be connected to an ordinary telephone socket, and a suitable lead should be supplied with the computer. This normally has a

*Fig.1.46 The modem port is below the left-hand
USB socket, and should not be confused
with an Ethernet port*

normal BT connector at the end which connects to
the wall socket, and the smaller type of telephone
connector that connects to the modem (Figure 1.47).
Unfortunately, the supplied leads are often quite
short, but a computer store or DIY superstore should
be able to provide a suitable extension lead if you are
"caught short".

The same sources can usually supply an adapter that
enables a telephone and a modem to be connected to
the same telephone wall socket. If you are lucky, the
lead supplied with the PC will have a built-in adapter

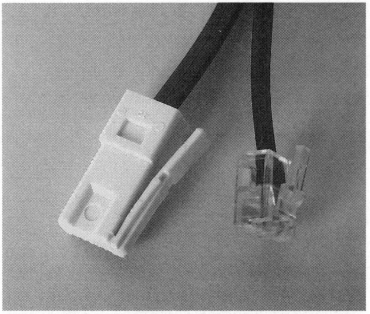

*Fig.1.47 The connectors of a standard modem
        cable*

(Figure 1.48). Note that only the telephone or the modem can be used at any one time. The ability to access the Internet even while someone else in the house is making a telephone call is a big selling point of broadband Internet services.

The connectors at both ends of a modem lead lock into the sockets, but it can be difficult to get the plug to fit securely into the modem's socket. Unless the plug locks into place properly it is unlikely that a good connection will be made. Pushing quite firmly on the plug will usually lock it in place. Some modem plugs and leads simply do not fit together reliably, and a replacement should then be obtained from the retailer

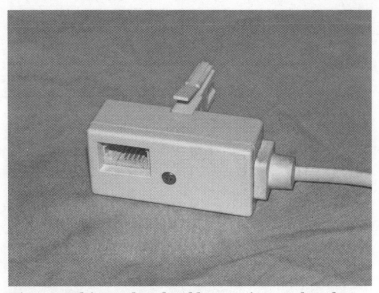

*Fig.1.48 This modem lead has an integral socket
for a telephone handset*

that sold you the PC. Remember to push the little
lever right down before unplugging the lead from the
modem. The plugs are often made from a fairly brittle
plastic and the lever is easily damaged.

Power

The order in which the various leads are fitted is not
usually of importance. The exceptions are the power
leads for the PC base unit, the monitor, and any mains
powered peripherals such as a printer and scanner.
These should be left until last. There is normally a
standard three-pin European mains connector on the

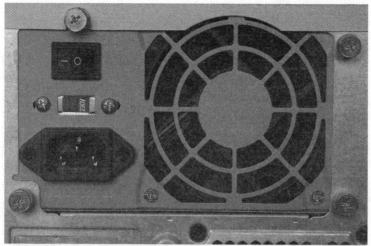

*Fig.1.49 Voltage selectors are now quite rare, but it
is as well to check for one, and that where
appropriate it has the correct setting*

rear of the PC (Figure 1.49), and the computer should
be supplied complete with a matching mains lead.

At one time it was the norm for a PC to have a voltage
selector somewhere close to the mains input
connector. The PC shown in Figure 1.49 does indeed
have a power supply unit that includes this voltage
selector, but it is something of a rarity these days.
Most PC power supplies will automatically adjust to
any normal mains supply voltage.

Where a voltage selector is present, it should be set
to the UK mains supply voltage by the manufacturer.
However, it is best not to make assumptions with this
type of thing, so look for a voltage selector on the rear
of the PC. If there is one, make sure that it is set for

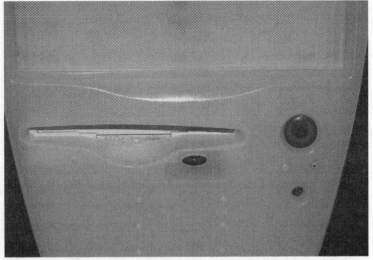

*Fig.1.50 The large pushbutton on the right is the
"on" switch, and the small one beneath it
is the "reset" switch*

operation at the UK mains potential of 230/250 volts.

There used to be a mains outlet on the PC that could
be used to power the monitor. This outlet was
connected to the mains supply via the PC's on/off
switch so that the monitor was switched on and off in
sympathy with the PC. The mains outlet is not
something you are likely to encounter these days, and
the on/off switching is handled in a different fashion.
Setting the on/off switch at the rear of a PC to the
"on" position only switches on the PC after a fashion.
It is unlikely that anything noticeable will happen
when the PC is switched on using this switch.

Switching on a PC is rather like switching on many

m o d e r n
television sets.
All it really does
is to put the
computer into a
sort of standby
condition where
it is ready to
start operating.
With   a
television set
you use the
remote control
to switch it on,
but unless you
have a media
PC it will not
have a remote
c o n t r o l .

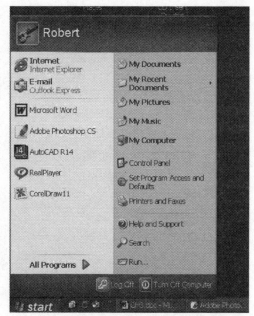

*Fig.1.51 The Start menu is used
when turning off the PC!*

Instead, it is switched on via a large pushbutton switch
on the front panel (Figure 1.50).

This switch used to have a toggle action. In other
words, you pressed it once to switch on the PC,
pressed it again to switch off the PC, operated it a
third time to switch the computer back on again, and
so on. This method is no longer used, and the action
of this switch when the PC is already on depends on
the way the PC is set up. It is possible that it will
have no effect at all, but it might provide a function
such as placing the PC into a semi-dormant state.

In order to switch off the computer you have to go to

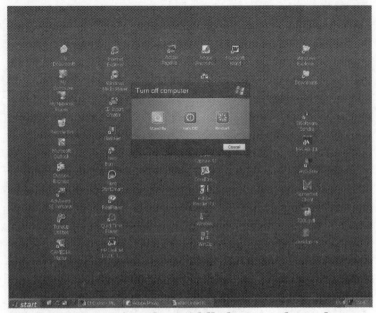

*Fig.1.52 Operating the middle button shuts down
Windows and the PC*

the Windows Desktop, left-click the Start button in
the bottom left-hand corner, select Turn Off Computer
from the menu that appears (Figure 1.51), and then
operate the Turn Off button in the new window that
is launched (Figure 1.52). Windows will then shut
down, and its final action will be to switch off the PC.
The large pushbutton switch is therefore more of an
"on" switch rather than an on/off switch, since you
never use it to switch off the computer.

There will probably be a very small button in addition
to this switch, and this is the reset switch. This should
only be operated if the PC has completely hung-up or

is otherwise out of control. Operating the reset switch has much the same effect as switching off using the main on/off switch at the rear of the PC, and then switching the PC back on again so that it boots into Windows again. Any work that has not been saved to disc will be lost if the reset switch is operated. It is usually made quite small and recessed into the case so that there is no risk of operating it accidentally.

Most PCs have at least two coloured lights on the front panel. The green one is just an on/off indicator that is switched on while the PC is powered-up and operating. It does not light up while the PC is switched on at the main on/off switch, and is otherwise inactive. The other light is usually red or red-orange in colour, and it switches on when a disc drive is being accessed. It will usually operate when any internal drive is active, with the only exception of the floppy disc drive. A new PC will not necessarily have a floppy disc drive as they are being phased out. Where one is fitted, it normally has its own built-in activity light.

Monitor power

CRT monitors have the same type of mains input socket as the PC, and the system should be supplied with a suitable mains lead. A flat panel monitor might have a normal mains input socket, but some of them are supplied with an external mains adapter. If there are other items of equipment in the system that use an external mains power supply, make certain that you do not get them swapped over.

Some adapters have a switch that enables various output voltages to be selected, or the polarity of the output voltage to be reversed. If any mains adapter in the system is of this type, read the setting up instructions for the equipment very carefully, and make sure that the settings are correct. Mistakes in the polarity or output voltage settings could cause costly damage.

The monitor should have a conventional on/off switch, but like the one on the PC, setting it to the "on" position only produces a standby mode. The monitor will only fully switch on when it receives a picture signal from the PC. The monitor reverts to the standby state when the PC is switched off and the video signal ceases. The monitor effectively switches itself on and off in sympathy with the PC.

If a PC will be left unattended it is good practice to switch off the monitor and the PC base unit using their main on/off switches. In fact it is probably best to unplug all the mains powered units in the system at the mains outlet. Probably few people actually do so, but there is some risk in leaving everything connected to the mains supply and to some extent still switched on.

I did come home on one occasion to find that the house was without electrical power. The power supply in a PC had developed a fault and had tripped the main overload cut-out at the fuse-box. No harm was done to anything other than the slightly scorched power supply that had to be replaced, but I suppose it might have been worse.

Points to remember

Modern PCs have three main units (base unit, monitor, and keyboard) plus a mouse, but they often come complete with other bundled units such as printers and loudspeakers. Carefully unpack everything and make sure that everything is present and correct, including all leads and documentation.

Most of the connectors used on computer leads will only fit if they have the correct orientation. The correct orientation is usually pretty obvious if you look carefully at two connectors. Brute force is unlike to have the desired effect when dealing with PC connectors, and could easily result in expensive damage.

Many PC connectors are colour coded so that it is fairly obvious as to which plug fits into which socket. The USB connectors on peripheral devices are not always the appropriate colour (black), but their flat shape means that there is little risk of confusing them with any other type of connector.

PCs are versatile devices that are designed to accommodate a wide variety of requirements. Do not worry if there are a number of connectors that are left unused. The PC I am using to produce this book is part of a comprehensive computer system, but it still has about half a dozen unused connectors.

PCs are often supplied complete with a built-in modem to facilitate a dial-up connection to the Internet. Most modems can also be used for sending and receiving faxes. A built-in modem is not suitable for any form of broadband Internet connection. The modem's socket is not usually in the main cluster of ports, but it will be somewhere on the rear of the base unit.

The main on/off switch is normally situated at the rear of the base unit's case. With this set to the "on" position, the PC is switched on by operating the large pushbutton switch on the front panel. Closing down Windows will automatically switch off the PC, which will actually go into a sort of standby mode.

The monitor will go into standby mode unless it receives a picture signal from the PC. Therefore, it effectively switches itself on and off in sympathy with the PC provided the on/off switch is left in the "on" position. The whole system should be unplugged from the mains if it will be left unattended for more than a short period.

Peripheral problems

Fair value

For many years, when you bought a computer you were very lucky indeed if it was supplied with a single peripheral device. In those days the world of electronics was very different, with a typical PC costing a few thousand pounds in today's money. Peripherals had equally high prices. After making adjustments for general inflation over the years, the cost of a budget printer back then was perhaps ten times as much as a modern low-end printer. Printers of yesteryear were possibly more strongly constructed, but their specifications were laughable by current standards.

These days it is quite normal for computers to be sold in the form of complete systems that include a range of what at one time would have been very expensive "optional extras". The extra items may be put forward as freebies, but the reality of the situation is that you are paying for them. In most cases these package deals offer very good value for money, but this is not something that should be taken for granted.

In particular, try to avoid buying systems that include relatively expensive items that are not really of any use to you. A "free" digital camera that really costs you fifty pounds or more is not really a bargain if you never use it. Another point to bear in mind is that the quoted values of freebies are often based on recommended retail prices. This is fair enough, but it is the actual shop price that should be used when gauging value for money. Most electronic gadgets are readily available at prices well below the recommended retail prices.

The likely reason that computer retailers like to sell you systems complete with various peripherals is that the lower cost of modern computers means a greatly reduced profit per computer. Selling lots of peripherals with each computer helps to keep the effective cost of each computer system high, with a correspondingly large profit per system. It also makes life easier for someone setting up their first computer system. Instead of having to build it up piece by piece, you have an instant computer system with just a single purchase.

However, it would be naïve to think that an "off the shelf" system will suit your needs as well as one that is specifically tailored to your requirements. Doing some research and buying individual units that precisely match your needs might be more time consuming and expensive than buying an "off the shelf" system, but it should still be the better buy. Perhaps the best approach is to buy a complete system from a company that offers some flexibility in the items that are included in the system. This should avoid wasting money on items that do not really "fit the bill", and are unlikely to be used much in the long term.

Mouse

These days every PC comes complete with a pointing device, which is usually a mouse. The mouse is often problematic when first using a PC. Either the pointer goes flying across the screen with the slightest of mouse movements, or a huge amount of movement is needed in order to make it move a significant distance.

The ideal mouse sensitivity is very much a matter of personal preference, and it also depends to some extent on the type of software in use. High sensitivity is suitable for most programs where the pointer will only be used to make menu selections. Low sensitivity is better in situations where very precise control of the pointer is needed, which mainly means graphics applications such as photo editing and technical drawing.

Windows enables the sensitivity of the mouse to be adjusted to suit each user's requirements. The first step is to go to the Windows Control Panel, and with Windows XP this often has an entry in the Start menu. This depends on the setup of the PC though, but there is an easy alternative route available. Double-click the My Computer icon on the Windows Desktop, and look at the left-hand column in the new window that

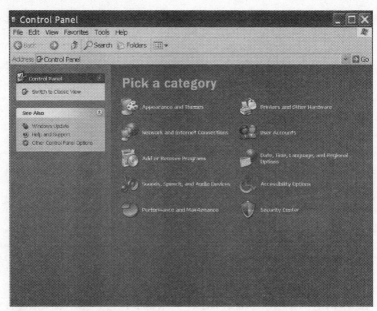

Fig.2.1 Initially the Windows Control Panel will look like this

appears. This should include a Control Panel link, and left-clicking it will launch the Control Panel.

Either way, the initial screen should look like Figure 2.1. The easiest way to access the window that controls the mouse functions is to first left-click the "Switch to Classic View" link, which is near the top left-hand corner of the window. The Control Panel should switch to look something like Figure 2.2, but the exact appearance depends on the hardware and software installed on your PC.

There will be either a straightforward Mouse icon, or one that mentions a specific make and (or) model of mouse. This depends on whether the PC is equipped

Fig.2.2 The Control Panel has been switched to the Classic View

with a Microsoft mouse, a generic type, or one of the more upmarket mice. In this case the mouse is a Microsoft type and double-clicking the Mouse icon produces the standard version of the Mouse Properties window (Figure 2.3).

Click speed

The slider control near the middle of the window is very useful. It enables you to adjust the maximum time that can be used between the two mouse clicks of a double-click. It is likely that a slower double-click speed is required if you find that double-clicks tend

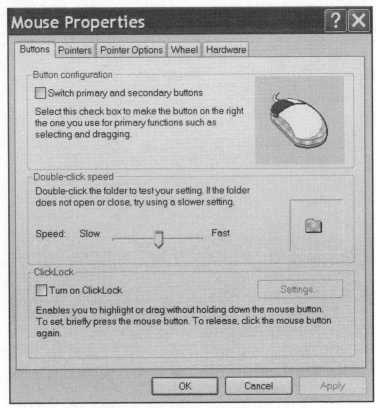

*Fig.2.3 The Buttons section of the Mouse
Properties window*

to be ignored by Windows. If double-clicks are still
ignored, either you are not releasing the button
properly after the first mouse click, or the mouse is
of low quality and it is not opening the switch contacts
even though you are releasing the button sufficiently.

The mice supplied with PCs are often of poor quality,
and many users replace them with one of higher

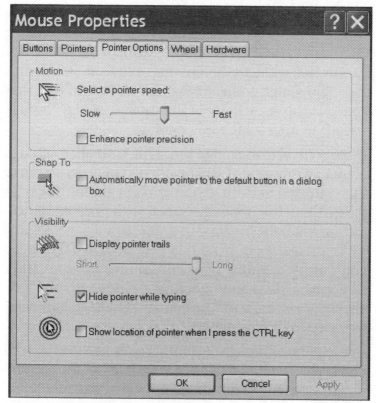

*Fig.2.4 The Pointer Options section of the Mouse
Properties window*

quality. Since you use the mouse a great deal in
modern computing, it makes sense to use one that
you find easy to use. These days a high-quality mouse
does not cost very much, and the one you discard may
well have cost you a matter of pence rather than
pounds. The same is true of the keyboard. If you will
be doing a fair amount of typing it makes sense to
buy a keyboard that you can use quite happily.

Returning to the subject of mouse sensitivity, the control for this is obtained by left-clicking the Pointer Options tab near the top of the window. The Mouse Properties window then changes to look like Figure 2.4. The slider control near the top is the one that controls the sensitivity of the mouse, or the "mouse speed" in Microsoft's terminology.

If the control is moved to the right, a smaller amount of mouse movement will be needed in order to move the pointer a certain distance. Moving the slider to the left has the opposite effect, with greater mouse movement being needed in order to move the pointer a certain distance. Note that you can move the slider control by placing the pointer over it and then dragging it to a new position. Alternatively, left-clicking to one side of the control results in it moving one step in that direction.

Finding the optimum setting is really a matter of trial and error. You have to be practical about things, and using a low speed setting is not very practical if you have only a very limited amount of space for the mouse. The mouse keeps running over the edge of its allotted area, making it necessary to keep picking it up so it can be repositioned near the middle of its operating area.

Windows provides a possible solution for those requiring precise control without having a large area for the mouse. In order to activate this facility it is merely necessary to tick the "Enhance pointer precision" checkbox. This is just below the speed control. The way this system works is very simple.

When the pointer is moved quickly, the mouse has its normal degree of sensitivity. This is made quite high so that relatively little mouse movement is needed in order to move the pointer around the screen.

When the pointer is moved slowly, the sensitivity is automatically reduced so that precise positioning of the pointer is much easier. This system relies on the fact that users tend to go much more slowly and carefully when trying to position the pointer very accurately, and it can be very effective. Having two mouse sensitivities is sometimes called "mouse acceleration" incidentally. There will be other differences if you are using a mouse that has its own property window rather than the standard Windows type. Essentially the same controls are always present though, and it should not be too difficult to find the ones you need.

Cameras

Two of the most popular peripherals for a modern PC are a colour printer and a digital camera. Even with quite low-cost cameras and inkjet printers it is possible to produce high quality pictures that will delight all but the most discerning of users. Although they are highly complex pieces of equipment, digital cameras have perhaps been less troublesome than most other types of peripheral. This is perhaps due to the fact that they are largely electronic and have relatively few moving parts. There is no film to load or to jam in the camera.

Fig.2.5 A Compact Flash card (left) and an XD card (right)

Despite their relative lack of problems, digital cameras can still provide a few headaches for the uninitiated. Digital cameras do not use film, but instead store the pictures on a special type of memory called "Flash" memory. Some cameras have a certain amount of built-in Flash memory, but it is more normal for the pictures to be stored on memory cards.

Unless you have bought an upmarket camera such as a digital SLR it is virtually certain that it will have been supplied with a suitable memory card. However, it is unlikely that it will be preinstalled. Memory cards vary somewhat in size and appearance, and two examples are shown in Figure 2.5. The larger card is a Compact Flash (CF) type, and these are popular for use in the larger digital cameras. The smaller

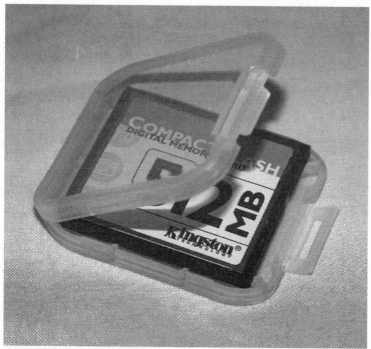

Fig.2.6 Put a memory card in its case when it is not in use

card is an XD type. These and other cards of diminutive dimensions are normally used in the compact digital cameras.

It is easy to overlook the smaller memory cards in amongst all the packing and other odds and ends that are included with most cameras, so be careful not to throw it away! If a case is included with the card (Figure 2.6), always keep the card in the case when it is not in the camera. The instruction manual for the camera should give concise instructions for fitting the card into the camera. It should involve nothing more

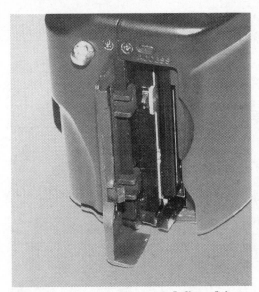

than opening a small door in the side of the camera, slotting the card in place (Figure 2.7), and closing the door again.

It is not possible to fit any memory card the wrong way round, but do make sure that it is fully pushed into place. If

Fig.2.7 A memory card fitted into its slot

you get an error message to the effect that no memory card is fitted, even though you just installed one, it could be that the card is faulty. It is far more likely that it is not fully pushed into the holder. The "hammer and tongs" approach is almost invariably the wrong one when dealing with electronic equipment, and it is always the wrong approach when dealing with delicate components such as memory cards.

If the card is reluctant to fit into place, you are trying to fit it the wrong way round, upside-down, or you are inserting it at an angle. Brute force will almost certainly damage the card and could easily render the camera a write-off. Fitting the card in place can be a bit fiddly, especially with the really small cards. However, with due care and a little patience, it should slot into place quite easily.

It is perhaps worth mentioning that the memory cards supplied with most digital cameras have fairly low capacities. This is fine if you only need to take a few photographs at a time, but it is of little use if you need to take dozens of shots before you will get a chance to upload them to a PC. Consequently, most users have to buy a much higher capacity card before they can use their new camera in earnest. There are half a dozen or more different types of card, so make sure that you obtain one that is compatible with your camera.

Storage and handling

It is definitely worth mentioning that memory cards are usually supplied with leaflets that give all sorts of warnings about careless handling. While Flash cards are perhaps a bit more hardy than these warnings seem to suggest, they are vulnerable to various types of damage. The thinness of most cards inevitably makes them a bit flimsy, and vulnerable to physical damage. Some cards are easily damaged by heat, but it is a good idea to keep any electronic goods away from sources of heat. This means that memory cards should not be left in direct sunlight, and the same also applies to the camera itself.

A memory card should not be inserted or removed when the camera is switched on. The camera might automatically switch off the memory slot when the door to the memory compartment is opened, but it is a good idea not to make any assumptions here. Make a habit of ensuring that any digital camera is switched off before fitting or removing a memory card. Last and by no means least, electronic components are easily zapped by static electricity. Flash cards have a degree of built-in protection, but it is advisable to keep them away from any known sources of large static charges. Even if a card survives a static discharge, there is a risk that any pictures stored on the card will be wiped and rendered unrecoverable.

Formatting

In the early days of digital cameras it was necessary to format a memory card before it could be used in the camera. These days you might find that the card works straight away when in is installed in the camera. When this happens, either the card has been supplied ready formatted, or the camera detects that it is unformatted and automatically formats the card. The card needs formatting if the camera's display says something like "FORMAT" or gives an error message to the effect that the card is faulty or needs formatting. You have to delve into the camera's instruction manual in order to find the routine for formatting a memory card.

The point of formatting is to provide a framework for the camera to work within when it is storing pictures. The information placed on the disc during formatting helps the camera to keep track of what is on the card,

*Fig.2.8 A miniature USB connector fitted to the
appropriate port of the camera*

and where it is on the card. Practically all modern
cameras use a system of formatting that is the same
as one used by Windows for hard disc drives. This
makes it easy to transfer files from a camera to a PC
that is running a modern version of Windows.

Some cameras are supplied with custom software
that is used to handle the uploading of images from
the camera to the PC. Many of these programs run
automatically when the camera is connected to the
PC. The normal method of connection is via a USB
port, but I have yet to encounter a camera that uses a
full-size USB connector. The small size of most

cameras makes a normal USB connector impractical, and a miniature type therefore has to be used. In Figure 2.8 the miniature USB connector is fitted into the camera. The larger connector on the right fits into a USB port on the PC. Apart from the fact it has a miniature USB connector, a digital camera is used much like any other USB peripheral.

When using custom software with a camera it is essential to read the documentation supplied with the software. The exact method of downloading and processing images varies significantly from one program to another. Not all cameras are supplied with custom software for downloading images, but instead rely on the built-in facilities of Windows. Even where custom software is provided, using the facilities of Windows is often available as an alternative.

As pointed out previously, memory cards are often formatted using a system that was originally designed for use with hard disc drives. As a result of this, a camera often appears in Windows as a disc drive. This makes it very easy to upload images to your PC, but it can be confusing for beginners, who connect their camera to their PC and find that nothing much happens. The image files on the card are actually accessible though, provided you know where to look for them.

It is worth bearing in mind that with most cameras it is not essential to connect the camera to your PC in order to upload some pictures. You can obtain card readers that plug into a USB port and enable a Flash

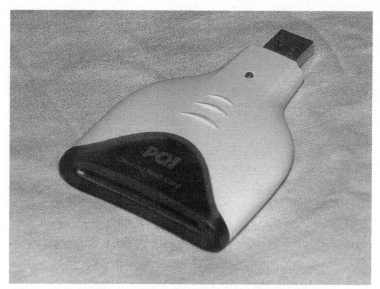

Fig.2.9 A USB card reader for Compact Flash cards

card to operate as a disc drive. It is clearly essential to obtain a card reader that is compatible with the particular type of Flash card you are using, but this should not be a problem. Readers are available for all the popular types of card, and some accommodate about half a dozen different types of card. The card reader shown in Figure 2.9 is for Compact Flash cards.

Note that some PCs have built-in card readers, and they are also included on some printers (Figure 2.10). In the case of printers, card readers are primarily included as a means of printing direct from a memory card, but the card can usually be accessed from the

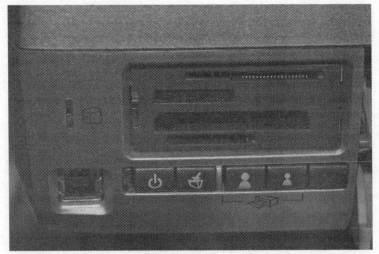

Fig.2.10 This printer has slots for various types of memory card

PC via the printer. However, you have to be careful not to accidentally press any buttons on the printer as this might initiate a print run!

On the face of it, there is little point in using a card reader of some kind when you can simply connect the camera direct to the PC. Bear in mind though, that connecting and disconnecting the camera can be a bit tedious. You have to be especially careful when disconnecting the camera, as this has been known to crash the PC. It depends on the particular setup you are using, but in most cases it is necessary to operate one of the buttons in the bottom right-hand corner of the Windows Desktop before disconnecting the camera. Where appropriate, the exact process should be explained in the camera's instruction manual.

By operating the button you are effectively switching off the camera and removing it from the system. This ensures that there are no problems when it is disconnected from the PC. Of course, this problem does not arise with some form of card reader, which can be left connected to the PC all the time. Another advantage of a card reader is that it can be used with Flash cards to provide additional data storage for your PC. Flash cards also provide a convenient means of transferring data from one PC to another. To a large extent, the old floppy disc drives have now been superseded by card readers and Flash cards.

Copy the files

With the Flash card connected to the PC via some form of card reader, accessing your picture files should be very easy. Windows identifies the drive by letters, with A and B being the floppy disc drives (if fitted). Drive C is usually the main hard disc drive, but it might be split into two or more logical drives (C, D, E, etc.) Any additional "real" hard disc drives come next, followed by CD-ROM and DVD drives. The card reader or camera will usually be the last in the sequence, possibly somewhere around drive F to H.

When using a new PC it is important to learn the identification letters for the various drives at an early stage. The built-in Windows Explorer program provides an easy way of looking at the drives installed on a PC and their contents. Double-clicking on the

2 Peripheral problems

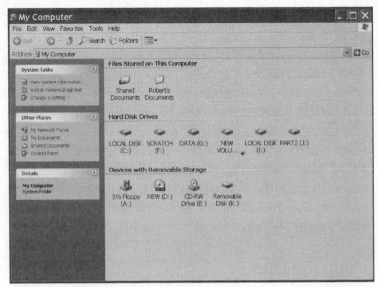

*Fig.2.11 The My Computer window shows all the
installed disc drives*

My Computer icon on the Windows Desktop will
launch Windows Explorer and it will show all the
computer's drives in the main panel (Figure 2.11).

The number of hard disc drives listed can be more
than the number of drives actually installed in the
computer. In fact this will usually be the case. The
very large hard disc drives used in modern PCs are
often partitioned to act as two or more separate
drives. In this example there are six notional hard
disc drives, but the PC only has two hard drives
installed. It is Removable Disk (K:) that is of interest
in this case.

It is a card reader that contains a Flash card that is
storing some image files. Double-clicking the entry

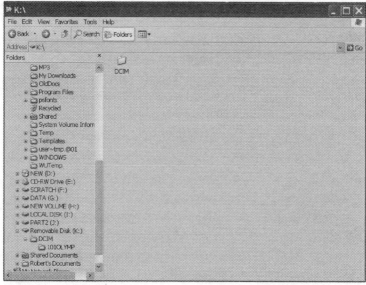

*Fig.2.12 The Flash card contains a single folder,
which in turn contains the images*

for this drive shows its contents, which is a single
folder (Figure 2.12). This is the folder placed there
by the camera's software, and double-clicking on the
folder showed that it contained another folder. The
way in which the contents of the card are organised
varies from one camera to another, but it is common
for a folder to be used as the main storage place, with
images then being grouped in subfolders of the main
folder. There could be a different folder for each day
for example.

In this example, double-clicking the single subfolder
revealed its contents, which was four image files.
There are various ways of copying files from a Flash

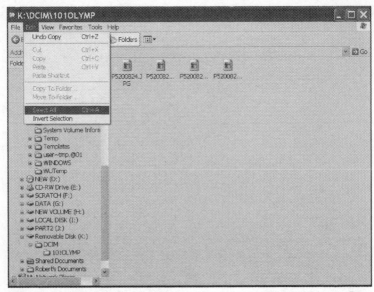

Fig.2.13 The Select All option is available from the Edit menu

card to a folder on a hard disc drive, but probably the easiest way is to first select all the files by choosing Select All from the Edit menu (Figure 2.13). Then right-click on an icon for one of the files to produce a pop-up menu, and select the Copy option (Figure 2.14). It does not matter which file you use when right-clicking. All the selected files will be copied, and not just the one used when right-clicking.

Having copied the files to the Windows Clipboard, navigate you way to the destination folder. Next, right-click on a blank area within the folder, and then select Paste from the pop-up menu that appears (Figure 2.15). The files will then be copied to the folder. In

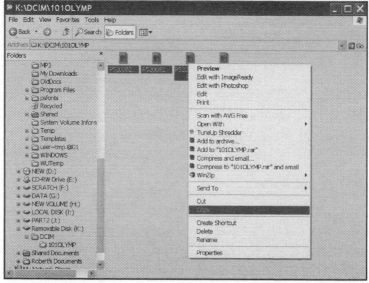

Fig.2.14 Select the Copy command from the pop-up menu

general, Flash cards are not very fast, so it could take several minutes if there are hundreds of megabytes of data to be copied.

Faxing

Many modems are supplied complete with fax software, and plenty of fax programs are available. Practically all modern modems can handle the sending and receiving of faxes, which uses a maximum baud rate of just 14,400 incidentally. In order to receive faxes the computer must monitor the telephone line via the modem. When a call is received it is answered by the modem, and the fax software

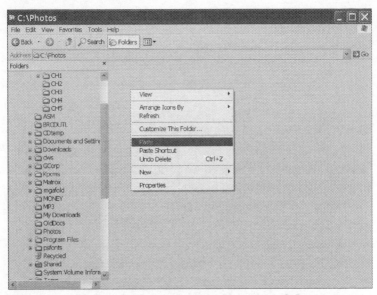

*Fig.2.15 Right-click in the main part of the
window and select Paste from the menu*

then controls things. The usual scheme of things is
for the software to automatically answer and decode
the fax, and it is then saved to disc in an appropriate
file format. Many of the early fax modems and
software packages lacked reliability, but modern
modems and fax programs are much better in this
respect.

Usually when I am asked for help with faxes, the
problem is sending them rather than receiving them.
The obvious approach to sending a fax is to run the
software and select the file you wish to send as a fax
from within the fax program. Although this may be
the obvious approach, it is not the way that most fax
software handles things.

There is a serious flaw in having the fax program process a file and send it as a fax. This will only work if the fax program can handle the particular file format involved, which in practice would tend to restrict faxing to a few popular file types. This type of thing tends to be a bit iffy in practice, because the file translation process is not always totally accurate. Matters are also complicated by the fact that there are numerous versions of most file formats. Each time a new version of a program is brought out, the file format changes slightly in order to accommodate new features.

Sending

The normal way of sending a fax is to use the Print command of whatever application software you used to generate the file. This command is available from the File menu in most Windows applications. The main advantage of this approach is that it avoids the file compatibility problems that would otherwise tend to plague the process of sending faxes. Another advantage is that it enables faxes to be sent from any software that has a Print command, which means virtually any Windows application software.

You are not limited to sending text, and there should be no difficulty in sending graphics or mixed graphics and text from photo-editing software, desktop publishing programs, etc. However, bear in mind that the print quality from a fax machine is likely to be inferior to the quality obtained when printing direct to a modern inkjet or laser printer. Sending a file as

2 Peripheral problems

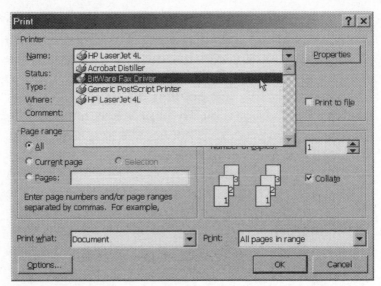

*Fig.2.16 The fax "printer" is selected from the
menu*

an Email attachment is the better option when the
highest possible print quality is required. Provided
the recipient is suitably equipped, they can then print
the file using their PC and printer.

Presumably the fax "printer" will not be the default
printer, and it must be selected before a fax can be
sent. Selecting the Print option will bring up a window
something like the one in Figure 2.16. The exact
appearance will depend on the version of Windows in
use and the application program being run. The
Printer section will show the default printer, but any
other installed printer can be selected using the pop-
down menu.

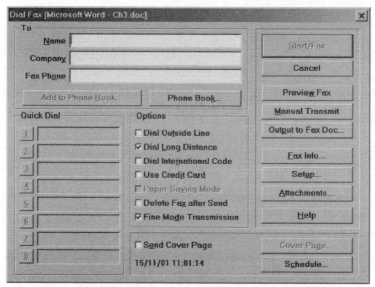

*Fig.2.17 Using the fax driver launches the fax
window from within the main program*

In this case it is clearly the fax option that must be
selected, and this should have been installed as part
of the installation process for the fax program. Other
options, such as the pages to print, are selected in
the usual way. Operate the OK button when
everything has been set up correctly, and the fax
program should then run (Figure 2.17).

The program in this example is the Bitware fax utility,
and there will be marked differences from one fax
program to another. However, it is a matter of
providing a few details such as the telephone number
to be dialled. Once this information has been
provided, left-clicking on the appropriate button sends

the fax. Most programs use status indicators and messages to keep the user informed about how things are progressing. Redialling is usually automatic if the number is engaged. Unless the link is lost during transmission of the fax, eventually there should be a message confirming that the fax has been sent successfully.

Printers

Many of the problems associated with printers are due to flaws in the driver software. Obtaining and installing new driver software is covered later in this book. Apart from driver difficulties it is mechanical problems that are most likely to occur. Getting the paper to feed through the printer correctly has been a cause of difficulties since the early days of PC printers, and it remains so.

Make sure that you read the manufacturer's recommendations, and that you adhere to them. Do not try to load more sheets of paper than the feeder is designed to accept, make sure that the paper guides are set correctly, and do not use paper of a type that the printer is not designed to handle. In particular, do not use paper that is thicker and heavier than the specified maximum for the printer. The normal paper path tends to be tightly curved, and using card or thick paper can easily result in the feed mechanism jamming.

Note that many printers offer an alternative feed path for thick media such as card and envelopes. The alternative path is usually straight, or something close to being straight, so that the media is not creased or crumpled on its way through the printer. Unfortunately, in most cases it can only handle one sheet at a time, so using the "straight" path can be time consuming.

Thin paper (about 90 gsm or less) usually goes through the feeder without any difficulty. There can be occasional problems with two sheets rather than one being pulled through the mechanism, but this is usually due to the sheets of paper tending to stick together. The paper tends to stick at the edges if it has not been cut to size quite as cleanly as it might have been. This problem can be reduced by running your thumb across the edges of a block of paper prior to loading it into the printer. In most cases this is sufficient to separate any sheets that are stuck together.

One of the most common complaints about inkjet printers is that they do not work properly if you load them with numerous sheets of photographic printing paper. In fairness to the printer manufacturers it has to be pointed out that many of the sheet feeders are only designed to take heavy photographic paper one sheet at a time. As explained previously, many printers offer a "straight" path for card and heavy paper. When using the thickest of photographic inkjet paper it is likely that this will have to be used. As always, read the printer manufacturer's recommendations and keep within them. If the paper should become seriously jammed, the printer's

*Fig.2.18 The tear-off strip must be removed just
before installing the cartridge*

instruction manual should give advice about
removing any pieces of media that are seriously stuck
in the mechanism. Prevention is better than cure,
and paper jams should be avoided as far as possible.
Repeated paper jams are likely to damage the
printer's paper feed mechanism.

Another common problem with inkjet printers is that
of the ink cartridges being loaded, but only blank
pages being "printed". In some cases the cartridges
are fitted, but the printer produces a message saying
that no cartridges are present. You can not totally
rule out a fault with the printer or the cartridges when

this happens, but incorrectly loaded cartridges are a more likely cause of the problem. Make sure that the cartridges have been fully pushed into their holders and clipped in place.

Ink cartridges are normally supplied with a tear-off strip that goes down one side and over the print nozzles (Figure 2.18). Its purpose is to prevent the ink drying and blocking the nozzles. The tear-off strip must be removed just before the cartridge is installed in the printer. Do not remove it any earlier, as this more or less guarantees that the nozzles will become blocked and that nothing will be printed.

Test cartridges

You might find that an inkjet printer works fine initially, but that you soon get warning messages to the effect that the ink cartridges are nearly empty. Alternatively, the printer might work fine for a few pages before running out of ink and producing some rather odd and incomplete results.

Printers are often supplied with "test" cartridges that have much lower capacities that the proper ones. These will become exhausted very quickly if you print full page colour photographs. Even when using full capacity cartridges you will probably get no more than about 20 to 40 full page colour photographs per set of cartridges.

The problem is often due to the printer's "fuel gauge" being inaccurate and indicating that a half-full cartridge is nearly empty. Do not replace a cartridge if the printer is producing good results. It is the quality of the prints that counts and not the amount of ink that the printer "thinks" it has in the cartridges. My current inkjet printer indicates that the cartridges are nearly empty after about eight photographs have been printed. It actually prints about 20 A4 photographs per set of cartridges. Inkjet cartridges are quite expensive, so throwing them away when more than half full is definitely not a good idea.

Inkjet printers normally use some form of calibration process to get the cartridges accurately aligned. In other words, the printer has to be adjusted so that the bits of the image printed in one colour match up properly with the bits printed in other colours. This process is sometimes fully automatic, but you have to load a sheet of paper into the printer so that it can produce a test sheet.

Some printers require manual calibration. This also requires a sheet of paper to be fed into the printer so that a test sheet can be produced. However, rather than electronics in the printer assessing the results, you have to examine the printout and enter the results into an onscreen form. Note that the printer will not produce optimum results unless the calibration process is carried out successfully. The calibration process must be repeated each time a new cartridge is fitted.

Scanners

Like printers, many of the problems encountered with new scanners are due to flaws in the driver software.

Also bear in mind the points mentioned in chapter one about making sure that any packing is removed from the mechanism, and that any locks are released. With a flatbed scanner it is essential that the glass is clean. Any sizeable dust particles will stick out on scanned images like the proverbial "sore thumb".

The control software for scanners can be quite complex to use. There is often a largely automatic mode, and it is a good idea to use this at first. Using an excessively high resolution is a common mistake when using a scanner for the first time. Scanning a full A4 page at 2400 dpi (dots per inch) should produce a first class image, but the resultant file would be large enough to make most PCs grind to a halt. Producing huge files can even result in the PC crashing. When doing large scans it is important to use the lowest resolution that will do the job well. Some experimentation will be needed in order to find the lowest usable resolution for a given application.

Monitor settings

Conventional monitors that use a CRT usually have a large number of adjustments available. These are normally accessed via a few pushbutton switches and an onscreen menu system. You have to consult the instruction manual to find out which functions are available on your particular monitor, and how the menu system works. The menu system is usually quite straightforward, but the range of available adjustments can be a bit bewildering.

There is usually a range of adjustments that can be used to counteract any problems with the geometry of the screen. It is advisable not to fiddle with these unless there is a very obvious problem that must be corrected. It is usually easier to make things worse than it is to cure the problem. Bear in mind that no matter how carefully the geometry settings are adjusted, you are unlikely to get anything approximating to perfection with this type of monitor.

The most important settings are the ones that enable the size of the image to be adjusted. Using the default settings it is normal for the picture to cover only about 60 percent or so of the screen. It is important to use something close to the full screen area in order to make a high resolution screen easy to read.

The usual arrangement is to have separate controls for vertical position, horizontal position, vertical size, and horizontal size. Start by using the positioning controls to get the picture roughly in the centre of the screen. Then use the size controls to make the picture as large as possible without losing anything off the edge of the screen. A little "fine tuning" should then get the picture fitting as accurately as possible. Finally, use the brightness and contrast controls to optimise the picture quality. Avoid having a very bright screen, as this can be fatiguing if used for more than short periods.

Points to remember

Windows provides various controls that govern the mouse and the onscreen pointer. The most important of these is the sensitivity (speed) control, and it is a good idea to try a range of sensitivities to find the one that best suits your method of working. If double-clicks are ignored by Windows, try using a longer double-click time.

Images can usually be uploaded to a PC via a USB link. A more popular method these days is to remove the memory card from the camera and fit it into a card reader. The card then appears to be a standard Windows disc drive, and its contents can be read in the normal way. Handle flash memory cards with care, and observe the manufacturers' warnings.

Modern printers are hi-tech gadgets, but the paper feed mechanisms are often pretty basic. In order to avoid paper jams you must stay within the manufacturer's recommendations about using card and heavy paper with the printer. If there is a "straight" paper path, use it when printing on the appropriate types of media.

Inkjet printers normally require calibration before they will produce top quality results. This is sometimes an automatic process, but it often requires a test sheet to be assessed manually. Calibration is required each time a new ink cartridge is installed.

Faxes are not normally sent by running the fax software and then indicating which file should be transmitted. Instead, the installation routine for the fax software installs a fax printer driver. Faxes are sent from within applications programs by "printing" to this device, which is selected from the list of installed printers. This enables faxes to be sent from practically any Windows application program.

The default settings of the monitor are unlikely to give anything approximating to the optimum settings with the video card in your PC. If you do not wish to get deeply embroiled with the numerous settings that are available, at least adjust the monitor for the largest possible picture, and for optimum brightness and contrast.

Updating and fixing

Is it working?

As those with many years of computing experience will testify, with a computer it is often a matter of opinion as to whether it is working. Some people consider that there computer is working properly despite the fact that it takes 15 minutes to boot up, and once booted into Windows it crashes at roughly 20 minute intervals! Others consider their PC to be faulty because it is 2 percent slower than they think it should be. Some would say that a slow booting and frequently crashing computer is fairly typical, but this is being very pessimistic about things. On the other hand, you are unlikely to get much pleasure from computing if you are a total perfectionist!

If your PC boots up reasonably quickly and works fairly reliably, then it is probably best not to start messing around with its settings and risk "rocking the boat". These days a boot-up time of less than a couple of minutes counts as reasonably quick. If the computer crashes or "freezes" very occasionally, but not often enough to be a significant nuisance, most

PC users would probably consider this to be "par for the course".

For those with little experience with PCs it is definitely advisable to put up with infrequent problems rather than taking the risk of making matters worse. The chances of an inexperienced user curing a very occasional problem are probably not that good. The chances of making things worse by persisting with attempts to find a cure are almost certainly much higher. Do not fall into the trap of blindly changing and messing around with settings in the hope that something will have desired result. This sort of thing is virtually certain to make a complete mess of the Windows installation before too long.

Major faults

Of course, if there is a major problem it must be dealt with. If everything is connected together properly, the PC is plugged in at the mains supply and the mains socket is switched on, there is a hardware fault if the PC does nothing or just produces a few beeps and goes no further. However, bear in mind that PCs often have two on/off switches. This was covered in chapter one, but it seems to cause beginners a lot of problems and it is worth covering it again here.

There is usually one on/off switch at the rear of the PC, and this is a true on/off switch. The PC can not work at all unless this is set to the "on" position. Setting this switch to the "on" position will not cause the PC to start its checking and boot-up sequence though. In order to make the PC start working it is necessary to operate a pushbutton switch on the front panel. There is often one large pushbutton and a small one. The large one is the on/off switch and the small one is the reset switch.

The latter should only be pressed if the computer hangs up completely and there is no way of regaining control. Operating the reset switch has much the same effect as switching the PC off and then back on again. It reboots and starts again from scratch. Any work that had not been saved will be lost. Fortunately, the computer freezing completely is relatively rare when using Windows XP. You clearly have to be careful not to accidentally operate the reset switch, but it is normally small and recessed into the front panel of the PC. You sometimes need to use something like a pen or pencil in order to press the button far enough to activate this switch.

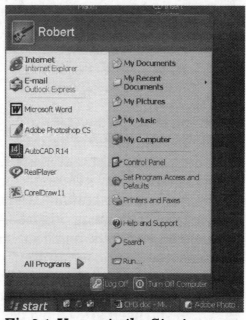

Fig.3.1 You go to the Start menu to switch off the computer

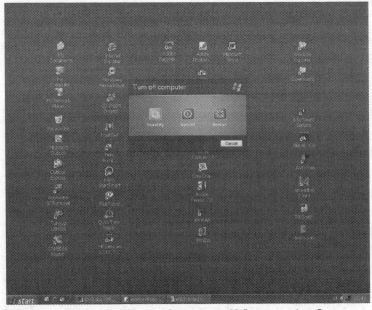

Fig.3.2 Operate the red Turn Off button in the middle to switch off the PC

When you have finished for the day you do not switch off the PC using either of the on/off switches. Instead, you operate the Start button in the bottom left-hand corner of the Windows Desktop, and then operate the Turn Off Computer button in the bottom right-hand corner of the Start menu (Figure 3.1). A small window will then appear in the middle of the Desktop (Figure 3.2), and you then operate the Turn Off Computer button. Windows will then close down and switch off the PC. Operate the pushbutton on the front of the PC when you need to switch it back on again.

Disc check

With versions of Windows prior to Windows XP it was quite common for a warning message to be produced during the boot-up sequence. The message would explain that the PC had been shut down improperly and that it was necessary for the hard disc drive to be checked for errors. The hard disc would then be scanned by a program called Scandisk, which was part of Windows in the pre-XP era. There were a number of things that could cause this message to appear, and it was often due to a program that had not shut down properly. It would also occur whenever the PC was simply switched off without shutting down Windows first.

Windows XP is less likely than its predecessors to do a scan of the hard disc during the boot-up sequence, and switching off the PC without first shutting down Windows is no longer guaranteed to have this effect. On the other hand, it could well have this effect, and is almost certain to do so if there is any hard disc activity when the PC is switched off. Windows has good reason for doing a check of the hard disc drive when the computer is rebooted.

One problem with switching off the computer while Windows is still running is that it tends to leave a variety of temporary files on the hard disc drive. These files are used by Windows and many applications programs as a normal part of their operation. The files are normally deleted by the program that generated them as part of its standard

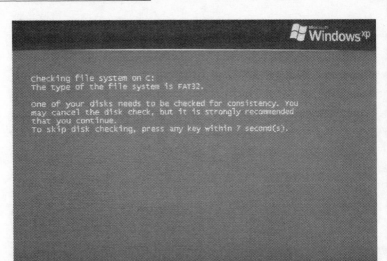

*Fig.3.3 You can press any key to skip the disc
        checking, but it is not a good idea to do so*

shutting down process. Simply "pulling the plug" on
the computer leaves these temporary files on the hard
disc, where they can mislead the operating system
and other software the next time the PC is used.

There is another problem that is potentially much
more harmful. Leftover temporary files can produce
some odd results but are unlikely to be too
troublesome. Switching off the computer while there
is some hard disc activity is a different matter. It is
almost certain to leave incomplete files on the disc,
and could damage the table that the computer uses
to locate files on the hard disc.

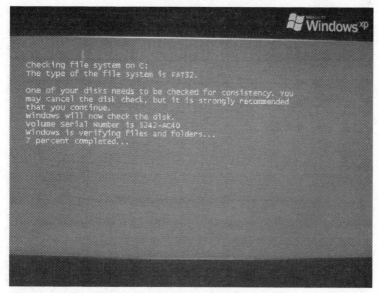

Fig.3.4 The files checking is underway

One or two errors on a hard disc drive can easily lead to several more errors, which can in turn lead to further problems. It is for this reason that Windows does its best to detect any hard disc irregularities, and to investigate any that are found. It is designed as far as possible, to locate and correct errors before they have a chance to multiply and get out of hand.

If Windows does detect a possible problem, a screen like the one shown in Figure 3.3 will appear in the middle of the boot-up sequence. With previous versions of Windows, many users would opt to abort the checking process, which was likely to be a false

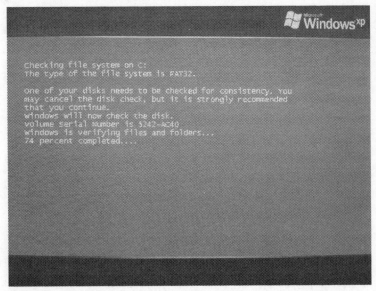

*Fig.3.5 Progress is slow, but at least no errors
have been detected*

alarm. There is a much greater chance of a disc error
if Windows XP detects a potential problem.
Consequently, it is definitely not a good idea to abort
the disc checking by pressing a key. Let Windows go
ahead and check for problems.

Provided Windows is allowed to proceed with the disc
checking, the screen will change to look something
like Figure 3.4. The bottom line of text lets you know
how far the process has progressed. Although the
program operates quite quickly, modern hard disc
drives have very high capacities. A few minutes after
the start of the disc checking the program has only
completed 74 percent of the task (Figure 3.5).

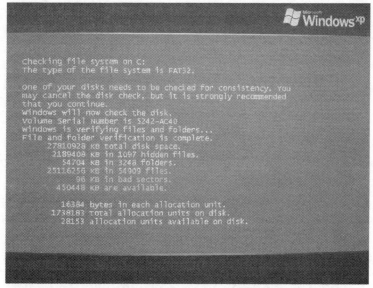

*Fig.3.6 The checking has been completed, and a
list of results are provided*

However, the good news is that it has not detected
any errors.

The program will list any problems that are found,
together with any actions it has taken to correct
matters. Note that it is unlikely that the program will
be able to fully repair any problems that are found.
Its aim is to make the disc usable and reliable again,
rather than to repair damaged files. Fully repairing
damaged files is probably not possible, because some
data is likely to have been lost when the PC was
switched off. In general, the program will recover
what it can, with any damaged file fragments being
placed in a folder on the hard disc called Found.

You can examine the contents of the files using a suitable program, but it is unlikely they will contain anything worthwhile. In most cases the damaged files will be ones used by the program, and they will not be your data files. Even if the damaged file or files did contain some sort of data, the chances of recovering significant amounts of valid data are probably quite small. Prevention is better than cure, and it is better not to invite trouble by switching off the PC other than by closing down Windows.

A screen like the one shown in Figure 3.6 will appear once the checking has been completed. This just gives a few basic facts about the hard disc plus the results of the checking process. Assuming the disc is deemed to be fully serviceable, Windows will then continue to boot in the normal way.

Typical faults

If a new PC clearly has a major fault it should be returned to the supplier. The only thing you are likely to achieve by delving into the PC is to invalidate the guarantee. Typical faults have the PC failing at some point during its initial test sequence, failing to start booting into Windows, "freezing" during the boot-up sequence, getting into Windows all right but then crashing, resetting, or behaving erratically, failing to do anything at all, or not producing any picture on the monitor.

You can try some simple checks yourself, just in case the problem is something fairly trivial. However, it is

*Fig.3.7 Some video adapters have two video
output connectors*

probably best not to try fixing a difficult problem if
you do not have much experience with PCs. The
chances of success are minimal. If there is no display
at all it is worth checking that the monitor is switched
on, plugged into the mains supply, and reliably
connected to the video output of the PC. A few video
cards have two outputs for monitors and can be used
with twin displays (Figure 3.7). In the single display
mode there will only be a signal from one of the output
sockets. Try using the other video output socket in
case this is the active one.

A monitor will only go from standby to the active mode
if it receives a proper signal from the computer.

Therefore, a lack of any picture is not necessarily due to a faulty monitor. Even in the standby mode, most monitors have an indicator light that comes on when it is plugged into the mains supply and switched on. If this fails to switch on, check that the mains supply is getting through to the monitor.

Try borrowing a mains lead from the PC base unit or another gadget and using it in place of the one supplied with the monitor. If you are using a multi-way mains board to provide additional outlets, try powering the monitor from a different socket. Some of these boards are a bit pernickety and not as reliable as they could be. Try powering the monitor direct from a mains wall socket. The monitor is almost certainly faulty if this fails to get any response from it.

PC or monitor?

You can save a certain amount of hassle by determining whether it is the PC or the monitor that is at fault. It avoids the need to return the PC base unit and the monitor even though only one of them is faulty. The "acid test" is to try it with another PC, but this will not be a practical proposition for everyone. This test is only possible if you have access to a PC that has the appropriate type of video output socket. If the monitor does burst into action when tried with another PC, clearly it is not the monitor that is at fault.

Some video cards have an output for use with a television set. This is really intended as a means of using games software with a large screen. The average television set, despite its large screen, does not give the sort of quality associated with computer monitors. However, many games operate at relatively low screen resolutions and therefore work quite well with a television set. Of course, many flat panel television screens provide high quality results, and some of these televisions are compatible with at least one type of PC video out.

Anyway, it might be possible to get a television set to act as a temporary monitor while the faulty monitor is repaired or exchanged. This depends on the specification of the PC and the television sets you have available, but it might be worth investigating. Even when you have a working monitor, the television might be better for some applications such as games.

If the base unit fails to do anything, the power lead swapping and other techniques used with a monitor can be used with the base unit in an attempt to make it to do something. There is almost certainly a major fault if it can not be persuaded to at least start the initial checking routine. It is not actually that unusual for a faulty PC to do nothing at all.

A PC's power supply unit has a number of safety features that are designed to protect the supply itself and the rest of the PC if a serious fault is detected. A major fault in practically any part of a PC might be detected by the power supply. If a problem is detected, the protection circuits will avoid further damage by not allowing the power supply to switch on.

Help

Most new PCs are supported by some form of Helpline provided by either the retailer or the manufacturer. It is worth giving this a try if it is free or reasonably cheap, but I would not spend pounds getting advice about a PC that is almost certainly faulty and will eventually have to be returned under guarantee. Take the PC back to the shop or arrange for its return if it was purchased via some form of distance selling (mail order, Internet, etc.).

Modern PCs are generally quite reliable, so unless you are very unlucky it should start up and boot into Windows without any problems. This is not to say that everything will be absolutely perfect thereafter. Odd and niggling little problems are the bane of PC users' lives. You might be in luck, or there could be odd problems when you use the PC in earnest. It is probably more likely that some odd little problem will occur before too long.

Software problems

The things that can go wrong are many and varied. One new PC I used seemed to work perfectly in every respect until I used it with a popular photo-editing program. It actually worked very well with this program until you zoomed in for a close-up view of part of a picture. Some parts of the picture then became a bit scrambled. If you tried to pan to a different part of the picture things became much worse. In fact the zoomed view became totally scrambled and useless. Since the pan and zoom facilities of the program were essential when doing practically any photo-editing, this rendered the program virtually unusable.

This type of problem where practically everything works but there is just one minor problem is fairly typical. The problems can be more major though, with perhaps a program tending to crash when you use the modem or a printer. Whether small or major, the cause of the problem is usually software related. Design errors in the hardware are not totally unknown, but are actually quite rare. Because the problems are mainly due to "bugs" in the software, they can be fixed by using fully working software instead.

These software problems occur in what are really three distinctly different types of software. They can occur in Windows itself, application programs such as games and word processors, and the hardware drivers. The latter seem to be the cause of most problems, and this aspect of things will be considered first.

In the pre-Windows era it was necessary for each program to be supplied with numerous hardware drivers so that it could operate with pieces of hardware such as high resolution displays and printers. The problem with this approach is that a vast number of drivers are needed in order to permit practically any program to work with virtually any piece of hardware. This was not very practical, and it meant that the chances of fully utilising a program with the PC you happened to be using were not very good.

Application software was often supplied with a range of built-in drivers for various items of hardware, which provided another chance to get your PC system fully working. Unfortunately, most application software was only supplied with drivers for the more popular items of hardware, and most hardware only came with drivers for the more popular pieces of software. Life was usually very difficult if you used anything other than mainstream hardware and software. Even if you did stick to mainstream products there was still a chance that you would make an unlucky choice.

An operating system like Windows eases the problem by providing a link between the application programs and hardware such as printers, the sound generator, and the video display. The hardware is supplied with a driver for Windows, and this integrates it with the Windows operating system. Once the hardware has become part of Windows, it should operate properly with any Windows program that could sensibly work with that type of hardware.

While this is fine in theory, in practice it is something less than perfect. The applications programs "talked" directly to the hardware with the old way of doing things. This gave optimum efficiency and enabled the relatively crude PCs of that era to run respectably fast. An operating system such as Windows becomes "the middle man", and inevitably slows things down as it reads the instructions from the application software and interprets them into something that will provide the desired effect from the hardware.

Most users were perfectly happy to accept a trade-off in performance for the convenience of needing a single driver for each piece of hardware. Modern PCs are much more powerful than the ones used in the early days of Windows. This renders any loss of performance due to the interpreting process of little importance in most applications. The reduction in performance is still present though, and it is unhelpful in applications where speed is of paramount importance.

The main problem with Windows drivers is not the loss of performance produced by this method, but the fact that they are usually very complex pieces of software. All the software coding has to be written to perfection or a "bug" of some kind will occur. This is actually the case with any type of software. However, the rules and regulations that govern the operation of driver software seem to be many and complex, making the task of writing driver software even more difficult and exacting than normal.

Many of the problems with drivers have been caused by two pieces of hardware in the PC being incompatible. This seems to be the result of one or both sets of drivers taking shortcuts that cause conflicts between the two items of hardware. The support sections of manufacturers' web sites often seem to contain plenty of advice about getting troublesome hardware combinations to work together in harmony.

Quick on the draw

Another reason for problems with driver software is that the hardware companies are keen to get their new products onto the market as soon as possible. They wish to gain a lead over their rivals, or maintain their lead if they are already the frontrunners. Waiting for 100 percent tested and reliable driver software to become available does not seem to be a priority. This can make life much more difficult for their customers.

It is now quite normal for new hardware to be released with drivers that contain a few bugs. On a couple of occasions I have purchased the latest thing in computer hardware only to find that the supplied drivers could not be installed at all! It was necessary to obtain updated drivers before the new hardware could be used. This is not really an acceptable way for a manufacturer to operate, but in the PC component business it seems to happen from time to time.

With some types of hardware it is quite normal for a succession of new drivers to be released after the initial launch of the product. In fairness, some of these provide new or improved features, or perhaps faster operation, rather than fixing bugs. If you can obtain a new driver that fixes a significant problem, it clearly makes sense to install it. The situation is different with new drivers that provide better functionality rather than bug fixes. Most computer users have tales of new and improved software that has actually

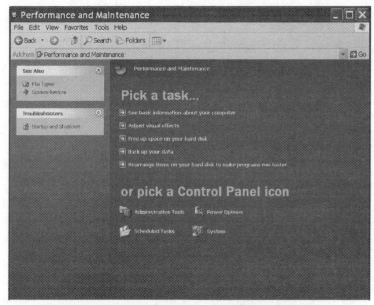

*Fig.3.8 The Performance and Maintenance
section of the Windows Control Panel*

been much less use than the previous version. Driver
software is certainly not immune from this
phenomenon. For inexperienced computer users it
is probably best to heed the advice of the old adage
"if it ain't broke, don't fix it". In recognition of the fact
that new drivers are not always quite as good as they
are supposed to be, Windows now has a facility that
makes it easy to go back to the previous driver.
Consequently, there should be a way back to normal
operation if you should happen to install a driver that
turns out to be a bit of a disaster.

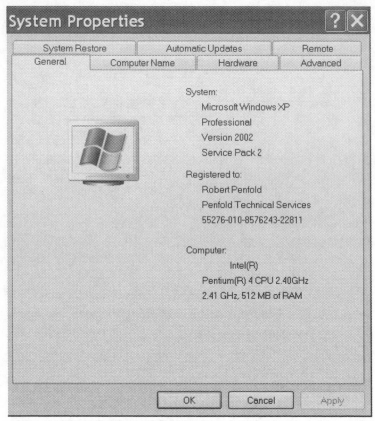

Fig.3.9 The System Properties window

Initial checking

If things to not seem to be quite right, it is worth going into a part of Windows called Device Manager. In this context the word "device" covers the majority of the PC's built-in hardware, including things that are on expansion cards, such as a modem or an upmarket

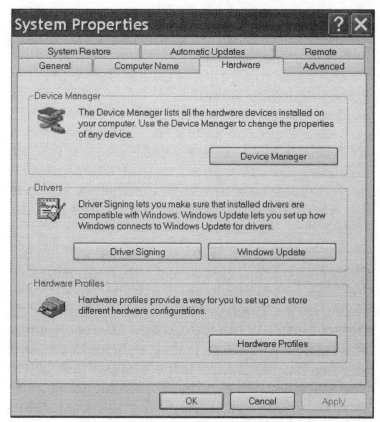

Fig.3.10 The Hardware section of the System Properties window

sound system. A certain amount of external hardware is also covered by Device Manager, including the keyboard and mouse. Things like printers and scanners are not included, but the ports that they connect to are covered by Device Manager.

The routes to Device Manager are all somewhat round-about in nature. Probably the easiest is to go to the Start menu and select the Control Panel option. In the Control Panel window, left-click the Performance and Maintenance link or icon, and the window will change to look like Figure 3.8. Next, left-click the System icon or link-text, and the new window of Figure 3.9 will then appear. In this case it is the Hardware section that is required, so operate the Hardware tab near the top of the window. Once in the Hardware section (Figure 3.10), operate the Device Manager button.

At last, the Device Manager window will appear (Figure 3.11). You could be forgiven for thinking that the designers of Windows have deliberately tried to make Device Manager difficult to get at. This is almost certainly the case, since Microsoft has a general policy of making things difficult to access if they can do serious harm to the Windows installation when misused. It is certainly possible to do more harm than good if you start playing with the settings in Device Manager. In fact it is likely that you will do more harm than good if you start playing with the settings, so do not do anything in Device Manager unless you are sure you know what you are doing.

There is no harm in looking though, and what you are looking for in Device Manager is yellow question marks or exclamation marks in the left-hand column. In this example there is a yellow question mark about two-thirds of the way down the list of entries. A question mark indicates that Windows has detected

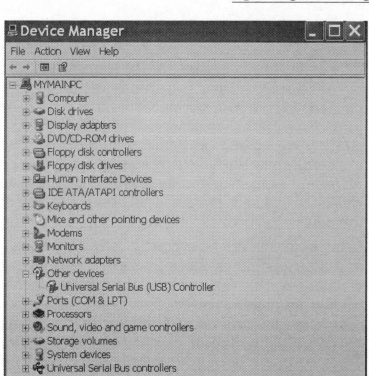

*Fig.3.11 At last, the Device Manager program is
launched. Practically all the PC's
hardware has an entry in the list*

that things are not quite as expected, and that there
is a possible problem. In this case the problem is
simply that a piece of hardware has been
disconnected from one of the USB ports. On booting
up, Windows has detected that this hardware is not
present, and it has therefore indicated a potential
problem in Device Manager.

A yellow exclamation mark is usually more serious. However, it is possible for everything to be working fine despite the fact that there are one or two errors indicated in Device manager. Windows can "think" it has found something wrong when there is actually no problem of any significance. Things also work the other way round, and the computer can have a serious problem despite the "all-clear" being given by Device Manager. Many hardware faults are not detectable by Device Manager, and it will not necessarily detect problems with drivers.

Many problems will be correctly picked up though, and an exclamation mark in Device Manager is definitely a cause for concern. If a problem occurs when using a certain piece of hardware, and Device Manager indicates a problem with the same hardware, then there is clearly something amiss. Things certainly need to be investigated if a new PC has one or more problems indicated in Device Manager. It is worth contacting the Customer Support department of the PC's retailer or manufacturer to see if there is a known problem and an easy solution. It is likely that there is a hardware fault if there is no known problem with the driver software. However, hardware faults are not very common, and there will probably be an easy solution.

Finding drivers

The appropriate customer support service for your PC should be able to supply any updated drivers that are required to get the PC into full working order. In the real world, you can often save yourself some telephone calls and a fair amount of hassle by searching for them yourself. Computer manufacturers often have a Support or Download section on their web sites where you can download the latest drivers for the hardware used in their PCs. In fact there is usually a facility of this type for any computer related device, including such things as printers, scanners, and digital cameras.

There is inevitably a delay between manufacturers of the hardware coming up with new drivers, and these drivers finding their way onto the web sites of PC manufacturers. A point you have to bear in mind here is that many PC manufacturers actually build relatively few of the components used in their PCs. In fact many PCs are actually assembled entirely from "off the shelf" components, with the manufacturer just doing an assembly job.

Consequently, it is often possible to obtain drivers earlier by going to the web sites of the companies that produced the individual components. Unfortunately, determining which hardware is used in a given PC can be a bit difficult. Your PC should really be supplied with a specification sheet that lists all the components that it uses, including the exact model of graphics card, soundcard, modem, etc. Delving into the interior of the PC to determine which components are present is probably not a good idea for those with little experience of PCs.

There is actually a useful facility built into Windows that can provide many details about the operating

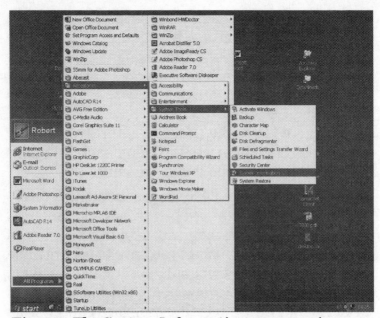

*Fig.3.12   The System Information program is
accessed via the Start menu*

system and hardware used in your PC. It is accessed
by going to the Start menu and selecting All Programs
– Accessories – System Tools – System Information
(Figure 3.12). The initial window will look something
like Figure 3.13, and it provides some basic details
about the operating system, processor, and amount
of memory fitted to the computer.

If you are concerned that you might have been "short
changed", and the PC might not have the right
processor or amount of memory installed, this section
of the System Information utility will provide the
answers. In this example the PC is equipped with an

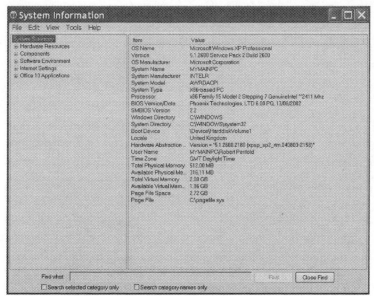

*Fig.3.13 The initial screen of the System
Information program*

Intel 2411MHz (2.41GHz) processor and 512
megabytes of memory. The genuine memory is
referred to as Total Physical Memory by the System
Information program. The virtual memory is actually
space reserved on the computer's hard disc drive,
and this is used when there is insufficient physical
memory. Things generally slow down a bit when a
PC starts using virtual memory.

The processor is actually a 2.4GHz type. There is
often a small discrepancy between the processor's
specified speed and the one reported by the System
Information program. It does not really matter
whether the processor is running slightly faster or

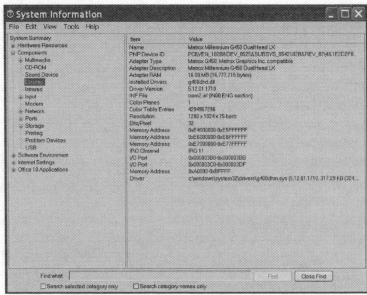

*Fig.3.14 Here the Components category has been
        expanded*

slower than its stated speed, or the program has made
a minor error when calculating its speed. A small
difference is of no practical consequence.

A large error could be due to the PC being set up
incorrectly, but it is more likely to be due to the
processor having an equivalent speed rating. In other
words, it runs at (say) 2.5GHz, but it is equivalent to
an Intel chip running at 3GHz. The manufacturer
therefore decides to call it a 3.0GHz processor rather
than a 2.5GHz for marketing reasons.

The System Information program has various
categories listed down the left-hand side of the
window, and left-clicking the little button to the left of

each category results in it being expanded (Figure 3.14). In this example the Components category has been expanded, and then the Display section has been left-clicked to select it. Details of the display hardware are listed in the right-hand section of the window. This shows that the display adapter is a Matrox Millennium G450, and it even gives the exact version of it (Dual Head LX). An entry lower down the list shows that the display adapter is fitted with 16 megabytes of video memory.

Windows update

If you do not fancy trawling the Internet in search of better drivers, there is a simpler alternative that you can try first. Windows has an automatic update feature, which will sometimes find and install more up-to-date drivers. This is not its primary purpose though, and it is mainly aimed at fixing any odd problems that users encounter with Windows. These days an equally important reason for having this feature is that it provides security updates.

Many viruses and worms are designed to exploit a security flaw in an applications program or the operating system itself. Sometimes these flaws have already been covered by software updates, but not everyone has bothered to update their PCs and the infection has been able to spread. In fairness to amateur PC users, there have been worms that have exploited old security "holes" in the operating systems of servers. The professionals maintaining

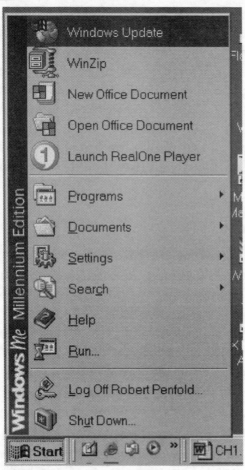

*Fig.3.15 Windows Update might
be in the Start Menu*

the affected servers had not bothered to routinely update their systems. Some worms and viruses exploit security flaws that were unknown up until that time, but patches to fix the problems are soon made available when this sort of thing occurs.

Anyway, the fact that you have a new PC with Windows newly installed does not mean that it is fully up-to-date. This depends on factors such as the age of the disc used to install Windows, and whether any updates were installed via the Internet as part of the installation process. In most cases the newly installed operating system will not have the latest updates, so it is worthwhile using the automatic update feature even if there are no apparent problems with the PC. This is especially important if you will be using the PC to access the Internet.

Depending on the version of Windows in use and the setup of your PC, it might be possible to launch the Windows automatic update facility via the Windows Update option in the start menu (Figure 3.15). More probably you will have to select Help and Support from the Start menu (Figure 3.16), and then left-click the Windows Update link in the new Window that is launched (Figure 3.17). This is the first option in the "Pick a task" section. Of

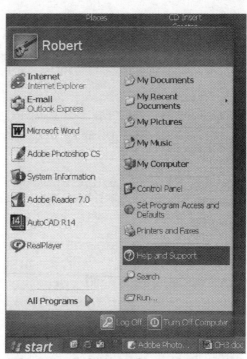

Fig.3.16 Select Help and Support from the Start menu

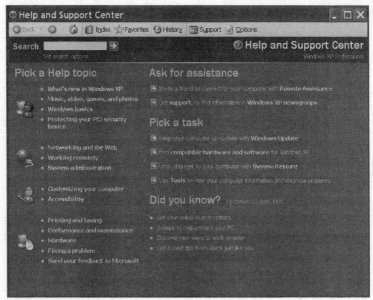

Fig.3.17 Left-click the Windows Update link when this new window appears

course, the PC must have an active Internet connection in order to use any form of online update system.

The Windows update system produces the Welcome screen of Figure 3.18, and the first step is to operate the Scan for Updates link near the middle of the page. The scanning process is usually quite quick and produces a list of available updates in the left-hand section of the screen (Figure 3.19). Left-clicking an entry brings up a list of available updates in that category. The list, together with details of each update, is displayed in the main section of the window,

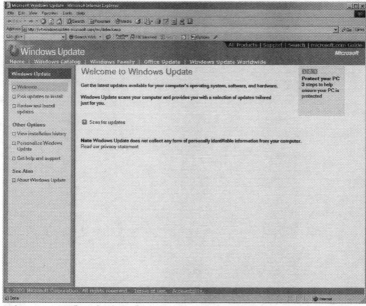

Fig.3.18 The initial screen of the Windows Update facility

as in Figure 3.20. In this example only one update is listed, but this is a security type that needs to be installed.

It is as well to look through the other categories to see if there is anything worth installing, but you will probably find that many of the updates are not of relevance to the Windows installation you are using. There might be foreign language updates for example. In the current context, if there are hardware driver updates you will presumably wish to select them. In the normal course of events though, you might prefer to leave well alone and not bother

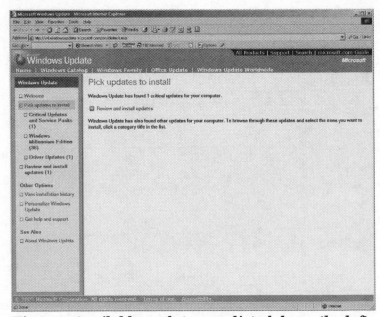

Fig.3.19 Available updates are listed down the left-hand side of the screen

with hardware updates. This depends on whether you feel confident about dealing with any problems that might arise as a result of updating the drivers. The situation is different with security updates, which should always be installed.

Having selected the required updates via the Add and Remove buttons, activate the Review and Install Updates link in the left-hand section of the window. Then operate the Install button in the main section of the window (Figure 3.21). The updates will then be installed and a small window will show how the process is progressing (Figure 3.22). Once the

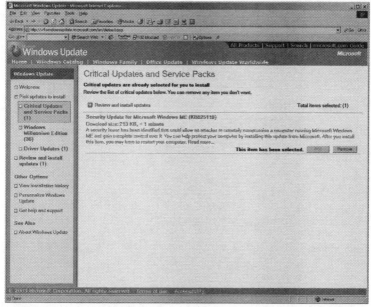

Fig.3.20 Available updates for a category can be detailed in the main part of the window

updates have been installed you will be asked if you would like to reboot the computer. It is not essential to do so, but the updates will not take effect until the computer has been rebooted.

Motherboard

There has been a trend in recent years to have as much of the electronics as possible on the main circuit board (motherboard), with relatively little provided by some form of internal expansion card. In particular, the sound and video systems are often part of the motherboard on modern PCs. The onboard

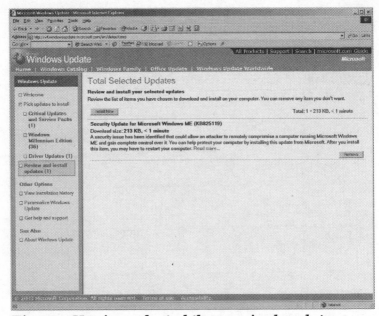

*Fig.3.21 Having selected the required updates,
operate the Install button*

sound and video circuits are usually produced under
licence by the motherboard manufacturer, or they use
chips provided by a specialist computer sound or
video company.

The drivers needed for integrated hardware are
usually available from the web site of the main board's
manufacturer. Additionally, they will probably be
available from the web site of the company that
originated the design. They will probably be available
from other sources as well. The real problem is in
determining the exact hardware used on the
motherboard so that you can obtain the correct

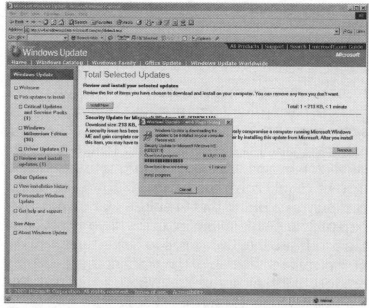

Fig.3.22 A small window shows how things are progressing

drivers. When looking for new hardware drivers it is always necessary to exercise due care or you could end up installing the wrong drivers. When dealing with hardware on the motherboard it is essential to take even more care.

Matters are not as straightforward as they might be when dealing with practically any item of computer hardware. Manufacturers of computer hardware tend to produce a number of products under similar names. What usually happens is that a manufacturer produces an item of hardware that becomes a big seller for them. They then launch further products with a similar name in an attempt to "cash in" on the success of the initial product. You can not really blame manufacturers for this ploy, since it makes good business sense.

It makes life difficult for users of these products, because having numerous products with virtually the same name makes it easy to download the wrong drivers. Installing the wrong drivers could make the computer unusable, although reverting to the original drivers should solve the problem. However, this is certainly something that should, as far as possible, be avoided. Some manufacturers have a section of their web site that is devoted to helping users make an exact identification of the particular version of a product that they are using. Where a facility of this type exists, it makes sense to use it.

If in doubt, it is best to let the Windows Update feature deal with driver upgrades, or to wait until the drivers appear on the web site of the PC manufacturer. It is likely that Windows or the driver installation program will detect that all is not well if you try to install an inappropriate driver. The process will then be halted before any damage is done. However, there is no guarantee that Windows or the installation program will come to your rescue.

Roll Back Driver

The Windows Roll Back Driver feature can be used when installing a new driver results in things going awry. This is really intended for situations where a

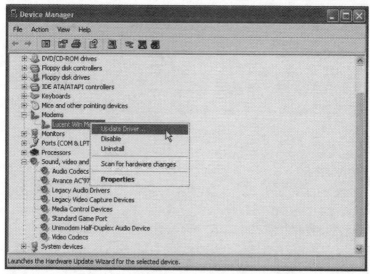

Fig.3.23 Right-clicking an entry produces a pop-up menu

driver upgrade does not work as well as it might, making matters worse rather than better. With luck, it will also restore normality when the new driver is not for the correct version of the hardware.

In order to start the Roll Back Driver process it is necessary to go into Device Manager and locate the entry for the appropriate piece of hardware. The next step is to right-click on this entry to produce a small pop-up menu (Figure 3.23). Select the Properties option, which will launch the properties window for the selected piece of hardware (Figure 3.24). The General section will probably be selected initially, so left-click the Driver tab near the top of the window to switch to the Driver section (Figure 3.25).

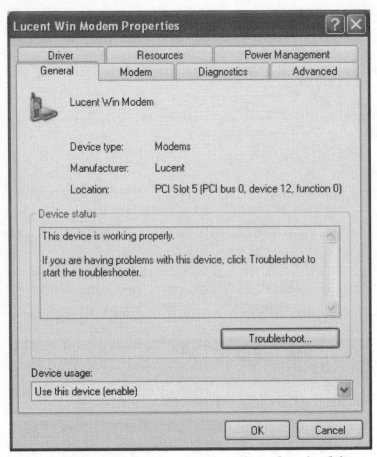

*Fig.3.24 The Properties window for what in this
        case is a modem*

Operate the **Roll Back Driver** button to start the
process of reverting to the previous driver. This
button will still be active even if the relevant driver
has not been updated successfully. However,
operating it will produce the warning message of

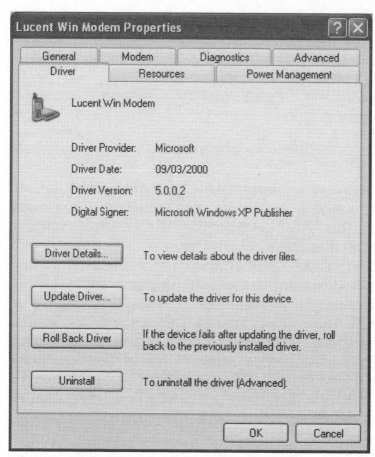

Fig.3.25 The Driver section of the modem's Property window

Figure 3.26. This gives the option of using the built-in Windows Troubleshooter facility to help locate and cure the problems with the device. Provided there is a previous driver to revert to, it is just a matter of answering Yes when asked if you wish to proceed, and letting Windows get on with it.

Lucent Win Modem

No driver files have been backed up for this device.

If you are having problems with this device you should view the Troubleshooter information. Would you like to launch the Troubleshooter?

| Yes | No |

Fig.3.26 This warning will appear if there is no previous driver to revert to

It is usually necessary to reboot the PC before changes to the system will take effect. The reason for this is that the changes will often involve settings stored in the Windows Registry. The Registry is a huge database of settings for Windows itself and practically any applications program. Some of these settings are dynamic, which means that they can be referred to at any time by Windows or an application program. Many of the settings are only used during the boot-up process, where Windows uses them to set a wide range of parameters. Consequently, changes to these settings will not take effect until the computer is rebooted.

Where it is necessary to reboot the computer in order to make changes take effect, Windows or the installation program will usually make this option available. Rebooting the PC could result in any unsaved data being lost from any applications programs that are running. It is good practice to avoid this possibility by saving your data to disc and closing all applications software prior to installing new software, upgrading drivers, or doing anything that might require the PC to be rebooted.

If it should be necessary to reboot the computer and this is not offered as an option by Windows or the installation program, manually rebooting the computer is a simple task. Go to the Start menu and select the Turn Off Computer option at the bottom of the menu. So far, this is the same as shutting down Windows, but in order to reboot the computer you must operate the Restart Computer button when the new window appears on the screen. This will result in Windows being closed down, but the computer will then start the boot sequence instead of switching off.

Driver installation

Windows has built-in facilities for adding device drivers, but few manufacturers seem to make use of them. Whether you are installing new hardware or upgrading drivers, it seems to be normal for the manufacturer to provide an installation program. This copies the device drivers onto the hard disc, and then the computer is restarted. The device drivers are installed automatically during the boot process. The manufacturer's web site should give concise information about installing the device drivers, and the installation instructions should always be followed "to the letter".

Note that the installation process is not always the same for each version of Windows, so make sure that you follow the instructions for the version of Windows you are using, and that you download the appropriate device drivers for this version. A new PC is almost

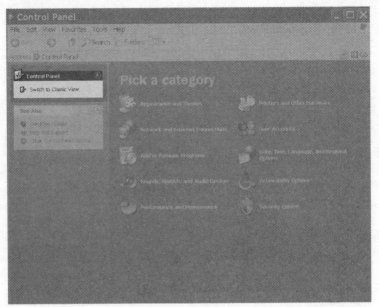

Fig.3.27 Start by switching the Control Panel to the Classic View

certain to be running Windows XP. As pointed out previously, Windows will probably refuse to install an incorrect driver, but it is best not to get into a situation where you are relying on Windows to prevent you from making a mess of things!

Automatic update

The method used to update application software depends on the particular program in question. Some programs have an automatic update feature, and a facility of this type is available for Windows XP. Turning on the Automatic Update feature of Windows is very easy, but you must be logged in as the

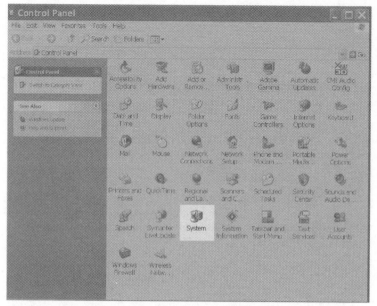

*Fig.3.28 Once in this version of the Control Panel,
double-click the System icon*

Administrator or be using an account that has administrator privileges.

Start by going to the Control Panel and left-clicking the Switch to Classic View link near the top left-hand corner of the window (Figure 3.27). The window should change to look something like Figure 3.28, but its exact appearance will depend to some extent on the hardware present in the PC and the software that is installed. Launch the System Properties window (Figure 3.29) by double-clicking the System icon, and operate the Automatic Update tab near the top of this window.

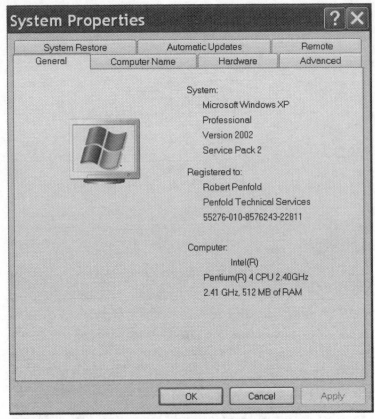

*Fig.3.29 The General section of the System
Properties window*

The window will change to look like Figure 3.30, and automatic updating is activated by left-clicking the Automatic radio button. By default the computer will look for updates every day. The drop-down menu on the left (Figure 3.31 gives the option of having the update performed once a week on the selected day.

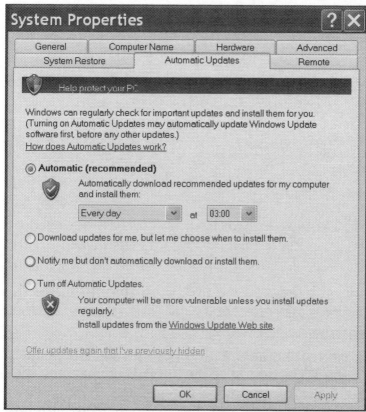

Fig.3.30 Operate the Automatic radio button in order to switch on automatic updating

The menu on the right gives a choice of 24 times in the day when the search for updates will be performed. It is important to select a time when the computer is likely to be switched on. Choosing a time such as 3-00 AM when the computer will always be switched off effectively disables the automatic updating. Having made the required changes,

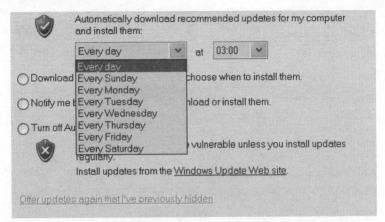

*Fig.3.31 A search for updates can be made each
day or on a certain day each week*

operate the Apply and OK buttons to make the
changes take effect and close the System Properties
window.

Of course, any automatic update facility is dependent
on the PC having an active Internet connection when
the search for updates takes place. This is not a
problem when using some form of broadband
connection, since it will be active whenever the PC is
switched on. Automatic updating works less well with
a dial-up connection, where there is a good chance
that the connection will not be active when the
searches take place. Also, any large downloads that
are required should not be a problem when using a
broadband connection. Large downloads might not
be a practical proposition when using a dial-up
Internet connection.

You need to be aware that the Automatic Update facility does not install every available update. It installs only those that Microsoft deems to be high priority or critical updates. This seems to mean any updates that fix potential security weaknesses, and those that fix serious bugs. Lower priority updates such as newer drivers and added features or improvements to Windows are unlikely to be installed automatically. Therefore, it is still necessary to use the normal updating facility from time to time so that you can select and install useful but non-critical updates.

Software update

Updating application programs can sometimes be done automatically, but this is by no means a feature of all programs. Where this feature is available it will probably handle nothing more than minor bug fixes. Minor version upgrades such as from version 7.0 to 7.1 are unlikely to be covered by an automatic update facility, and will have to be handled manually.

Major upgrades from (say) version 7.21 to version 8.0 are not usually made available as free upgrades. For this type of thing it is normally necessary to purchase the upgrade version of the program, which could be pretty expensive. In general, it is best not to habitually buy program upgrades. The cost can start to mount up, eventually dwarfing the original purchase price of the programs. Only buy upgrades if they provide new features that are genuinely useful to you, and they represent reasonable value for money.

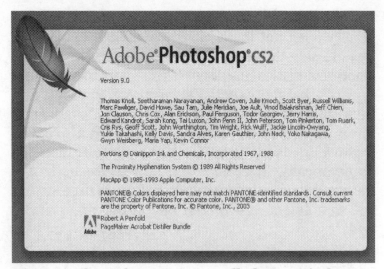

Fig.3.32 The Help system usually has a window
that shows the version number

Note that the application software bundled with PCs is sometimes a sort of second-class version. Some features may be limited or missing. Even if it is a fully featured version of the program, it might not be possible to upgrade it when a new version comes along. I suppose that this is reasonable, given that you have probably paid very little for the bundled software. On the other hand, one might have expected the software companies to gleefully accept all the upgrade business they could get. Apparently, selling version upgrades is the way in which they obtain most of their income.

An automatic update facility is still very useful even if it only handles a few bug fixes. The way in which automatic updates are handled varies from one

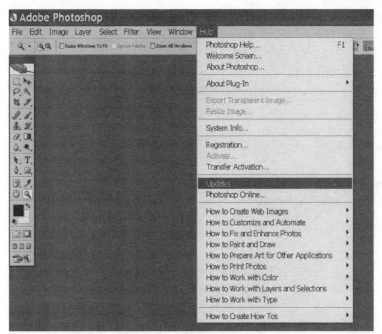

*Fig.3.33 Photoshop CS2, like many modern
programs, has an Updates option in the
Help menu*

program to another, and it is something that is often
enabled or disabled when the software is installed. It
should be possible to alter the automatic update
settings once the program is installed. For manual
updates it is a matter of going to the web site of the
software company and looking for any updates in the
Support or Download section of the site. If you find a
likely looking update, it should be accompanied by
detailed download and installation instructions.

Before looking for updates it is more than a little
helpful to know the exact version of the program that

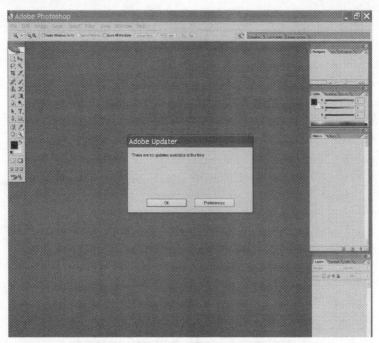

Fig.3.34 Updates are usually installed automatically, but in this case there were no available updates to install

you are currently using. This will often be displayed on the welcome window that is displayed while the program loads, and this window can usually be brought onto the screen via the Help menu. There will usually be an "About" menu entry, or a menu entry called something like "About" followed by the name of the program. Figure 3.32 shows the Welcome window for Adobe Photoshop CS2, and in this case is states near the top of the window that it is version 9.0 of the program.

Fig.3.35 This Preferences window is used to control automatic updating

Some programs have a built-in Update facility, and this is usually accessed via the Help menu. As can be seen from Figure 3.33, Photoshop CS2 has an Updates option in its Help menu. Selecting this option results in the program searching the Adobe web site for updates. With a facility of this type it is normal for any suitable updates to be installed automatically, but in this case no new updates were found (Figure 3.34).

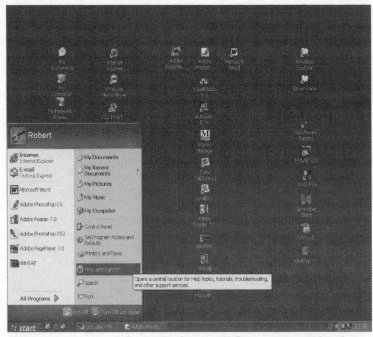

Fig.3.36 Access the Windows Help system via the Help and Support option in the Start menu

Operating the right-hand button in Figure 3.34 opens the Preferences window that is used to control the automatic updating facility (Figure 3.35). This is the same window that appears during the program's installation process. It enables this feature to be enabled or disabled, and you can opt to have updates installed automatically or only if you give permission. Photoshop CS2 is supplied complete with three additional programs, and you can select which of the programs utilise the updating facility.

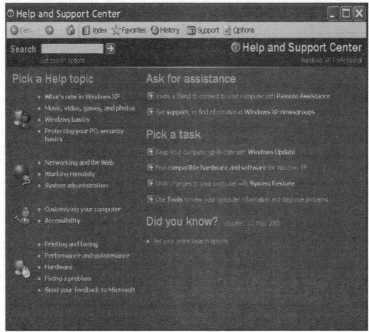

*Fig.3.37 The initial screen of the Help and Support
Center acts as a gateway to general
and more specific assistance*

Troubleshooter

Windows XP has a massive built-in Help system that
can be of use when trying to sort out a wide range of
problems. You can go direct to the Help system by
selecting the Help and Support option from the Start
menu (Figure 3.36). The initial screen of the Help
system looks like Figure 3.37, and a lot of general
assistance is available via the various links. The links
in the bottom left-hand section of the window are the
ones of most use when trying to solve problems.

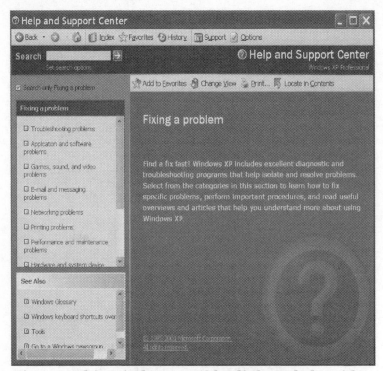

Fig.3.38 This window provides links to help with various types of Windows problem

The "Fixing a problem" link is the obvious place to start if you are experiencing a difficulty with Windows. This switches the Help and Support window to look like Figure 3.38, where there are links for Windows problems of various types. Figure 3.39 shows the Help screen for problems related to the computer starting up and shutting down. One of the links on this screen is for a Windows Troubleshooter that is designed to help with problems when starting up the computer or shutting it down.

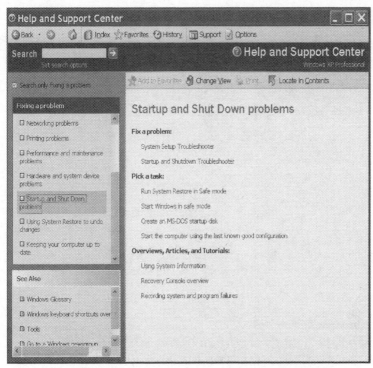

*Fig.3.39 This screen provides help with problems
when starting Windows and shutting it
down*

Suppose that you are having problems getting the
computer to close down properly. Instead of closing
down and switching off the PC, Windows instead
"freezes" with the closing down screen displayed, and
leaves the computer switched on. Operating the link
for "Startup and Shut Down problems" produces the
first page of the appropriate Windows Troubleshooter
(Figure 3.40). After reading the notes in the upper
part of the window, the lowest of the three radio

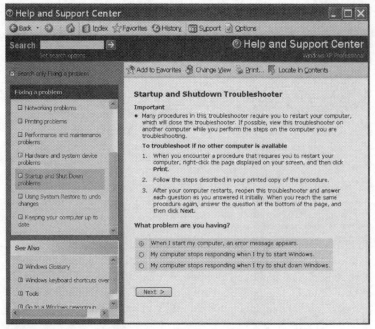

Fig.3.40 The first screen of the Startup and Shutdown Troubleshooter

buttons at the bottom of the screen would be selected and the Next button would be operated.

The troubleshooting process gets underway at the next screen (Figure 3.41), with a cure being suggested. After trying the cure you operate the appropriate button at the bottom of the page. One slight snag with this approach is that it can be necessary to close the Help and Support system in order to try some of the suggestions. You then have to go back into Help and Support and work your way through to the point where you left off. This type of

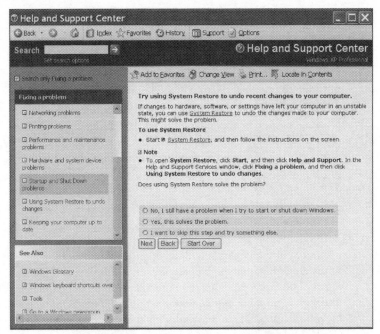

*Fig.3.41 This screen suggests a possible cure,
which you try before moving on to the
next suggestion*

troubleshooting system is much easier to use if you
have another computer. You can then run the tests
on the problematic PC while following the instructions
on the other PC.

The first suggestion in this case is that the System
Restore feature should be used. This takes Windows
back to its state at an earlier date when it was working
properly. This is a very useful feature, but it is not
applicable to a new PC that has no earlier and fully
working state to go back to. The bottom radio button
would therefore be selected, and the Next button

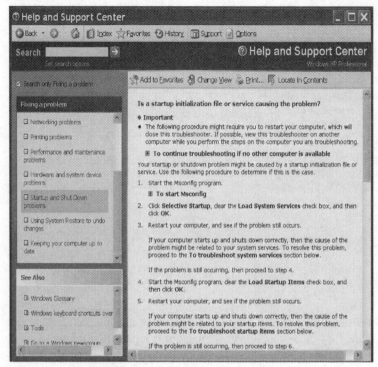

Fig.3.42 The first suggestion in not applicable in this case, so things are moved on to the next screen

operated to take things on to the next page (Figure 3.42). You continue working through the suggestions in this manner until the problem is cured or the Troubleshooter runs out of ideas.

Some of the suggestions can be quite involved, but you do not have to try any "cures" that you do not feel confident to undertake. The chances of success are better if all the relevant suggestions are tried, but it

*Fig.3.43 The homepage of Microsoft's online Help
and Support Center*

is better to skip one or two rather than risk doing serious damage to the Windows installation. The troubleshooter will provide an appropriate warning if a recommended course of action is a bit risky.

Of course, there is no guarantee that a given problem can be cured with the aid of a Windows Troubleshooter. With an obscure problem there is probably little chance of success. On the other hand, it does enable inexperienced users to go through the standard test procedures and rectify the more

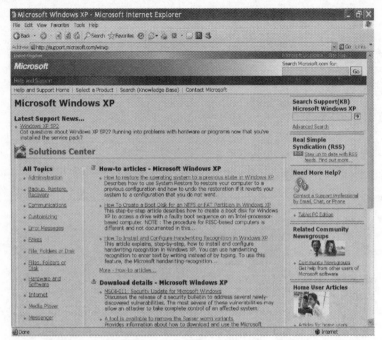

Fig.3.44 The homepage of the Windows XP online Help and Support Center

common problems. This will probably get things sorted out in the majority of cases.

On the Web

There is a vast amount of Windows documentation available at the Microsoft web site. It has to be admitted that much of this information is aimed at intermediate and advanced users, and definitely not at beginners. Even so, it might be worth looking for assistance on the Microsoft web site, especially where

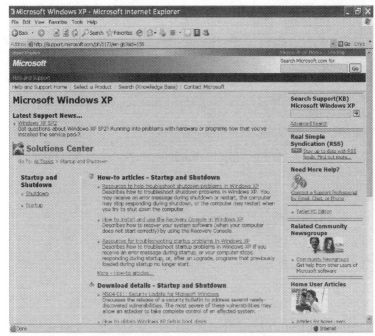

Fig.3.45 The page that gives access to help with problems when starting and closing down Windows XP

the problem is something fairly obscure in nature. This is the place to start if you wish to look for help on the Microsoft web site:

http://support.microsoft.com/

The left-hand column of the initial screen (Figure 3.43) enables you to select support for one of Microsoft's products, and in this example the Windows XP link has been right-clicked. This produces the initial Windows XP support page (Figure 3.44), and this has various topics listed in the left-hand column. There

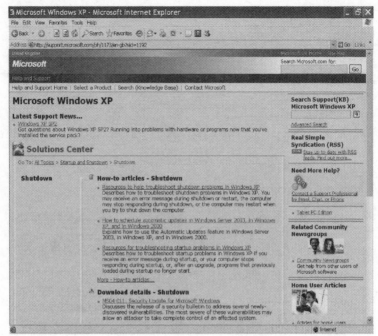

*Fig.3.46 This section is specifically for problems
when trying to get Windows XP to shut
down correctly*

is a link here for problems when starting up and
closing down Windows XP, and operating it produces
the page shown in Figure 3.45. Here it is possible to
select help specifically for problems when starting
Windows XP, or when shutting it down. Using the
Shutdown link produces the new page shown in
Figure 3.46. Here you can select an article from the
middle column of the page and then display it (Figure
3.47).

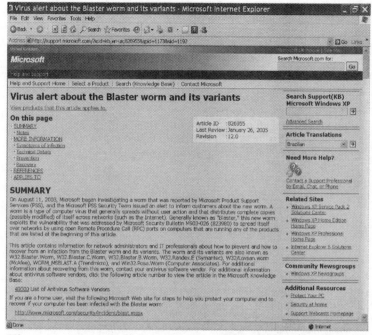

*Fig.3.47 An article has been selected from the list
and it is displayed in the browser*

There is, of course, a search facility. Just type a likely
search term into the Search textbox and then operate
the Go button. In Figure 3.48 I searched for help using
"codec" as the search term, and several articles on
this topic have been found. A codec (coder-decoder)
is sometimes needed when playing media files on a
computer, and there are several articles that cover
the use of codecs with Windows XP. You may not
always be successful with the search system, but it is
certainly worth trying.

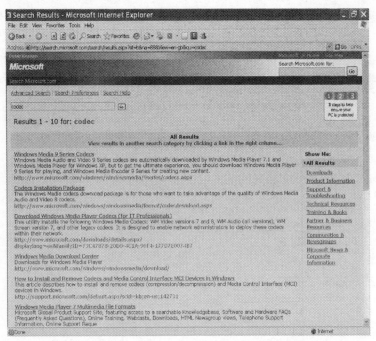

*Fig.3.48 A search for information about codecs has
produced a numer of articles related to
this topic*

Points to remember

Unless your PC has totally hung-up, do not switch it
off by cutting of the power. It should only be switched
off by closing down Windows, which will switch off the
PC for you. If a PC is shut down correctly, is possible

that Windows will scan the hard disc for errors when it is rebooted. It should be allowed to do so, since one or two small errors can mushroom into a major problem. The scanning program will usually fix any problems that it finds.

Once a new PC has been set up and is working, there can still be the odd problem or two. These can be caused by the Windows operating system, application programs, or by the hardware. It is probably not worthwhile putting much time and effort into curing minor niggles. There is little to gain in fixing them, and persistent attempts at finding a fix could make matters worse.

Practically every piece or hardware needs a program called a driver in order to make it work properly with Windows. Drivers are used by internal hardware such as sound and video circuits, and by external gadgets such as printers and scanners. Driver software is probably the most common cause of minor problems with a new PC. Fortunately, a search of the Internet will often locate updated drivers that will cure the problems.

Windows has a facility for automatically updating itself via an Internet connection. This only covers the updates that Microsoft considers to be "critical", which generally means security updates and fixes for serious bugs. There is also a manual updating facility, and this can be used to install various updates including improved hardware drivers.

Those with limited experience of dealing with PCs should think twice before installing an update that provides new facilities rather than fixing problems. In fact all PC users need to carefully consider whether this type of update is worthwhile. If your PC is working well and doing everything you need, there is a lot to be said for leaving it that way. In this context, "new" and "improved" do not necessarily mean that your PC will be more reliable.

When having difficulties with your PC, do not overlook the fact that Windows has a built-in Help system. This can provide help with a huge range of Windows problems, and it also includes a great deal of information about using the Windows operating system. It is effectively a built-in instruction manual.

The Help system gives access to the Windows Troubleshooters, which can also be accessed from other parts of Windows such as Device Manager. A Troubleshooter gives you a series of things to try, and one of these will usually get a "run of the mill" problem sorted out. Some of the more advanced methods suggested are not well suited to beginners, but you can skip any steps that you do not feel confident to tackle.

Windows problems

Activation

When you buy a PC it usually has the Windows operating system preinstalled, although preinstalled often means partially installed. The buyer often has to complete the installation process, but this should not require any technical expertise. The process is largely automatic, and you normally have to supply nothing more than a few personal details. Some suppliers "go the whole hog" and provide the PC set up and ready to run.

This makes it difficult to give helpful advice about any initial setting up, since the process varies considerably depending on the make and model of PC. There should be a "Quick Start Guide" or something of this nature to take you through the process in easy stages. Your PC might genuinely be supplied in a ready to run state, but having everything set up for you by the supplier usually costs a fair bit extra. Anyway, you have to "play it by ear" when dealing with the initial setting up.

Once the computer is "up and running" there will probably be a few tasks to complete before it is fully ready for use and just the way you would like it to be. Product activation is problem you are likely to encounter with Windows XP, which is the version now installed on all new PCs. Unlike previous versions of Windows, registering the program is not optional. Strictly speaking, it is not necessary to register Windows XP in order to go on using it indefinitely. It is the Windows Product Activation (WPA) that is essential, but this is normally done as part of the registration process.

In effect, the Windows XP operates initially as a fully working 30-day demonstration version of the operating system. This is the same for any retail copy of Windows XP, whether it is preinstalled or it is purchased separately and installed by the user. Normal single-user versions of Windows XP will only

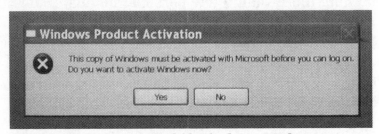

Fig.4.1 You are warned if Windows XP has not been activated

go on working if the product activation process is completed. If you ignore the onscreen warning messages and do not go through the WPA/registration process, the operating system will refuse to boot properly.

Windows problems 4

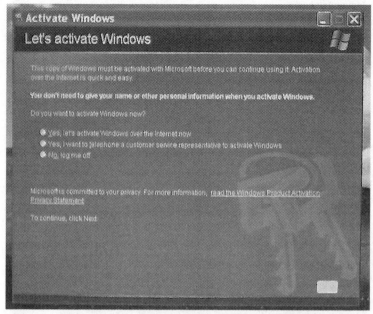

Fig.4.2 Where possible, opt to activate Windows
via the Internet rather than by telephone

All is not lost if you reach this stage, because it is still possible to go through the WPA/registration process and get the operating system working again. When you try to boot into Windows a message like the one shown in Figure 4.1 appears. In order to go on using the operating system it is necessary to operate the Yes button and proceed with the WPA process. Note that you can not log on to Windows by selecting the No option. You can only log off and shut down the computer if this button is operated.

Having opted to go ahead with the activation procedure, the window of Figure 4.2 appears. This

187

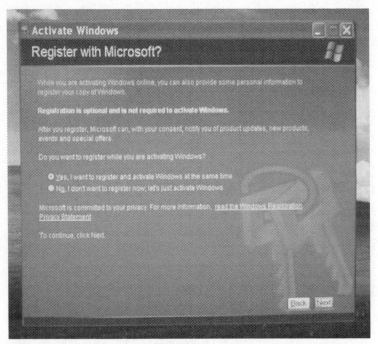

*Fig.4.3 You can activate Windows, or activate it
and register at the same time*

gives the option of registering by telephone, over the
Internet, or halting the activation process and logging
off. It is definitely a good idea to use the Internet
option if the PC is suitably equipped, since this is
much quicker and easier than verbally exchanging
multi-digit product keys and activation numbers over
the telephone. It virtually guarantees that the process
will be free of errors and will work first time. The
Internet method is the only one that we will consider
here, but the program provides full instructions if you
have to use the telephone route to activation.

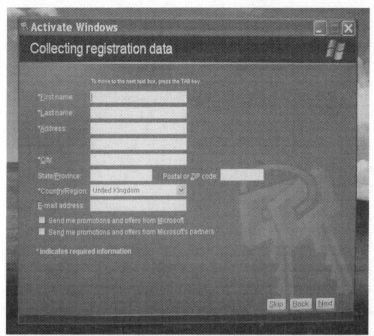

Fig.4.4 Your registration details are entered using this screen

After selecting the required option, operate the Next button to move the process on to the next window (Figure 4.3). This gives the choice of activating the program, or activating and registering it at the same time. The obvious choice is to activate the program and also register it while you are at it. If this option is selected, at the next screen the usual registration details are entered (Figure 4.4). Moving on to the next screen (Figure 4.5), your country is selected from the pop down menu and your telephone area code is entered in the textbox.

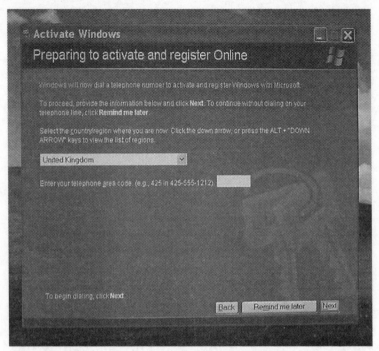

Fig.4.5 This screen is used to select your country and telephone area code

Operating the Next button brings up the window of Figure 4.6, and the program dials the server. The activation and registration processes are fully automated, and after a minute or two the screen of Figure 4.7 should appear, indicating that both processes have been completed successfully. After operating the OK button to close this window, the PC is ready for you to log-on to Windows.

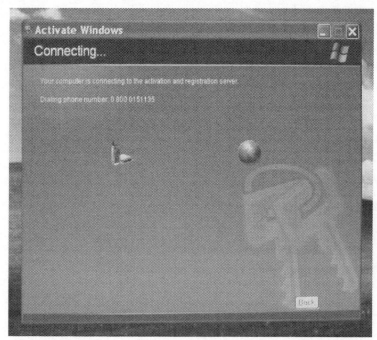

Fig.4.6 Windows dials the server and completes the activation process

Anti-piracy

The introduction of Windows Product Activation was, to say the least, a bit controversial. New users could be forgiven for wondering why this rigmarole is necessary. The idea is to prevent casual piracy of the XP operating system. However, like most anti-piracy systems, it does not make life any easier for legitimate users of the product. It can make life very much more difficult for legitimate users, although it will not necessarily do so.

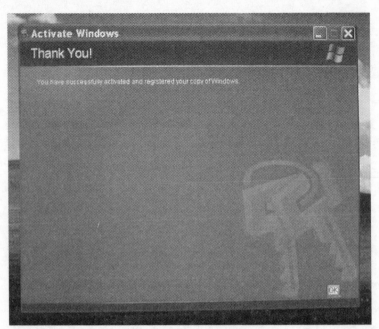

Fig.4.7 This screen indicates that activation has been completed successfully

As pointed out previously, a new installation of Windows XP is effectively just a 30-day demonstration version. Entering the product identification number during installation was sufficient to get earlier versions of Windows fully working, but with Windows XP it is only the first step in the activation process. You are locked out of the system if you do not activate Windows within 30 days of installing it, so you have to activate Windows or keep installing it from scratch!

Where possible, it is definitely advisable to opt for automatic activation via the Internet. The telephone alternative requires you to read a 50-digit code to a

Microsoft representative. This code appears onscreen during the activation process. This is bad enough, but you then have to enter a 42-digit code supplied by the representative. This is clearly an awkward and time-consuming way of doing things, and there is plenty of scope for errors to occur. By contrast, activation over the Internet is quick and there is virtually no chance of errors occurring.

WPA problems

Having to go through the WPA process should be no more than a minor inconvenience, and it is not the necessity for activation that is the main "bone of contention". The activation key is derived from your Windows product identification number and the hardware installed in the PC. To be more precise, it is these items of hardware that are used to produce the number:

Microprocessor type

Microprocessor serial number

Display adapter

SCSI adapter (if fitted)

IDE (hard disc, etc.) adapter

Network adapter (if fitted)

RAM amount

Hard drive

Hard drive volume serial number

CD drives

When Windows XP is booted, as part of the boot-up process the installed hardware is checked. The boot process is only completed if the installed hardware matches the full product key that is stored on the hard disc drive during the activation process. On the face of it, two computers having identical hardware could use the same activation key. In practice, this is not possible because the network adapter and processor serial numbers are unique. Two seemingly identical PCs would actually need different activation keys due to the processors and (where appropriate) the network card having different serial numbers.

There is a potential problem, in that any changes to the hardware will cause a mismatch during the checking process at boot-up. This problem is not as great as it might seem, because you are allowed a certain amount of leeway. Up to four of the items of hardware listed previously can be altered without the need to reactivate the operating system. If more than four items are changed, the activation mechanism will probably assume that the system has been copied to another computer, and it will halt the boot process.

This does not mean that you will have to buy Windows XP again. It will be necessary to call the WPA clearinghouse though, in order to obtain a new activation key. Frequent changes to the computer's hardware and calls to the WPA centre would presumably result in Microsoft refusing to provide further activation codes.

You are permitted four changes to the hardware in 120 days or less. This suggests that you can make as many changes to the hardware as you like provided they are made slowly so that there are no more than four changes in each 120 day period. I have not tested this in practice though. In practice there is little likelihood of problems unless your PC is given a massive hardware upgrade. A call to the WPA centre should then get things working again.

Bundled Windows XP

Product activation is always required when using a retail version of Windows XP. In other words, activation is always needed if you buy a boxed version of Windows XP from a computer shop, or if it comes bundled with a PC. It makes no difference whether you use the full version or an upgrade, the activation rules are the same. Note that a "boxed" version of Windows may actually be supplied with a PC as a shrink-wrapped product rather than a boxed type. However, if you have the proper Windows XP installation disc, it is effectively a full retail boxed version.

The situation is different with some bundled versions of Windows XP. Rather than using product activation the program is licensed for use with one PC. That PC is the one with which the operating system was supplied. This system usually works by having the program read the serial number of a computer chip in the PC. The operating system will fail to work unless the correct serial number is found, making it unusable on any other PC.

Not having to bother with product activation is a definite advantage, but these bundled versions of Windows do have a couple of drawbacks. Firstly, a major upgrade to the PC, or trying to eventually move the Windows installation onto a new PC, is likely to result in Windows refusing to work. Secondly, upgrades to newer versions of Windows are not always made available to users of bundled Windows installations. This might seem to be a bit unreasonable, but bear in mind that a bundled version of Windows is usually much cheaper than its full retail equivalent.

Fig.4.8 There should be a Control Panel entry in the Start menu

It is perhaps worth mentioning that product activation is not unique to Windows XP. It is also required with some of Microsoft's application programs such as the popular Office suite, and some other manufacturers use similar systems. If you use a PC at work it is quite likely that you will not have encountered product activation. PCs covered by volume licences usually run a slightly different version of Windows XP that does not require product activation.

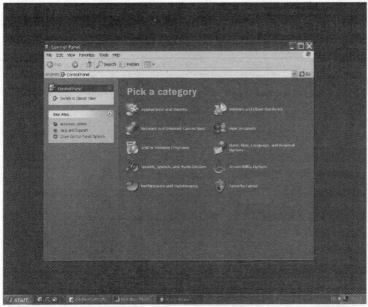

Fig.4.9 The initial version of the Windows Control Panel

Video settings

As supplied, the video system should do a reasonably good job with Windows itself, and with most application programs. The screen settings are often quite conservative though, and it can be advantageous to alter them. The first task is to launch the Windows Control Panel. The available routes to this built-in Windows program depend on how Windows is set up, but with a new installation there should be a menu entry for it in the Start menu (Figure 4.8). Left-click the Start button in the bottom left-hand corner of the Windows Desktop, and then

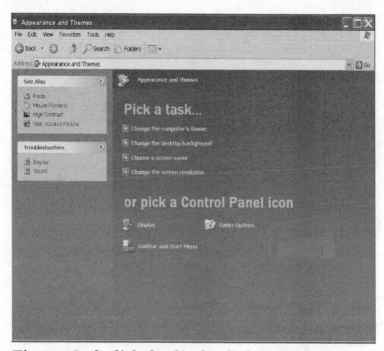

Fig.4.10 Left-click the display link in the bottom part of the main panel

left-click the Control Panel entry. A new window containing the Control Panel should then appear (Figure 4.9).

Next, left-click the Appearance and Themes link at the top left-hand corner of the main panel. This will change the Control Panel to look like Fig.4.10. Here you must left-click the Display link in the bottom section of the main panel, and this will launch a small window (Figure 4.11). The Display Properties window is extremely useful, and it provides tremendous control over the appearance of Windows. Since many

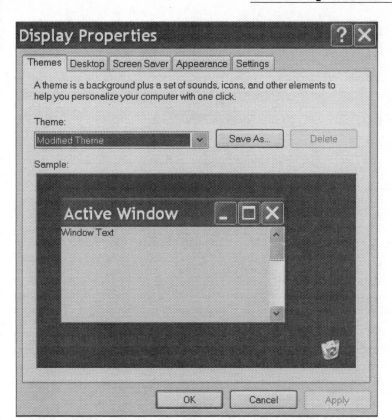

*Fig.4.11 The Themes section of the Display
Properties window*

application programs have their appearance based
on the colour schemes, etc., of Windows, this utility
also governs the appearance of most of the programs
that you will be using.

The Display Properties window has five sections, and
the Themes section is selected by default. The
controls that we require are obtained by left-clicking

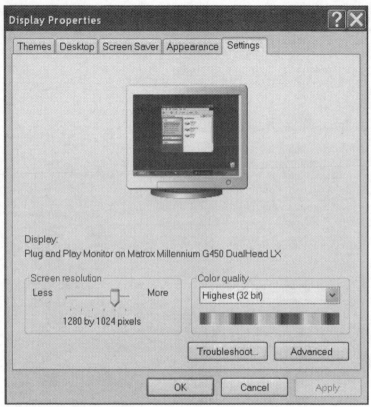

Fig.4.12 The Settings section of the Display Properties window

the Settings tab near the top right-hand corner of the window. This changes the window to look something like Figure 4.12. The Screen Resolution slider control can be used to adjust the horizontal and vertical resolution of the screen, and there will typically be about half a dozen combinations on offer.

A computer's display is produced from thousands of tiny dots, or pixels as they are called. It is a sort of high-tech mosaic. Screen resolution is specified in terms of the number of pixels used. With a screen resolution of (say) 1024 by 768, there are 1024 pixels in each row, and 768 rows. This gives 786,432 pixels in total, which might sound a lot, but this is about the minimum that will give good results with modern software.

Opinions differ about the ideal screen resolution, but it is dependent on the type of software you will be running and the characteristics of the monitor you are using. In general, higher resolution is better, but only if your monitor can handle it properly. High resolution requires a large monitor so that you can see everything clearly. Even for those with good eyesight, a small but highly detailed screen is difficult to use. Using a PC is likely to be very tiring if you have to strain your eyesight in order to see the screen properly. It could be harmful to your eyesight as well. Choose a resolution that is not a strain for you or your monitor.

Scan rate

The scan rate used by the monitor is also an important factor. The picture on the monitor is updated at a rate that is usually between about 50 and 100 times per second. This is normally called something like the "scan rate" or "refresh rate", and is given as a frequency in hertz. A scan rate of 75 hertz (75Hz) for example, means that the picture is updated 75 times per second. You will probably find other frequencies mentioned in monitor specifications, but the scan rate is the only one that is of importance to most users.

In the past it was quite common for monitors to have impressive maximum resolutions, but these could only be achieved by resorting to quite low scan rates. This usually gave a picture that had a noticeable flickering, making these monitors difficult to use for anything other than short periods. Modern monitors are generally better, but the scan rate could still be less than ideal at the higher resolutions.

Even if the scan rate is high enough for good results, it does not necessarily follow that the picture quality will be good enough. When used at maximum resolution, many monitors lack the definition needed to produce a really "crisp" picture. When using conventional monitors it is really a matter of using the "suck it and see" method to determine which screen resolution gives the picture that you consider to be the most usable. In the end, this is a purely subjective matter and the theory counts for nothing.

The situation is a bit different with flat-panel monitors, as these are designed to operate at a particular screen resolution. It is not a good idea to use a different screen resolution unless there is a good reason for doing so. Some games only operate at relatively low resolutions, or operate too slowly if used with a high resolution display. Apart from games, there is little modern software that is fussy about the screen resolution used.

A slight problem with some flat-panel monitors is that they do not handle fast movement very well. For example, an onscreen object moving quickly across the screen can tend to leave a slight and brief trail. With many types of software this is not particularly noticeable, but it can very apparent with some games or when playing videos on a PC. This is just a characteristic of some monitors and there is nothing that can be done about it.

Colour depth

Colour depth is just a fancy term for the number of colours that can be displayed. This is a factor that is governed by the display adapter in the PC rather than the monitor, although with flat-panel screens the monitor might be the limiting factor. There is usually a choice of three colour depths on offer from the Color quality menu near the bottom right-hand corner of the Display Properties window (Figure 4.13). These are 16, 24, and 32-bits, but there could be some lower options as well. This table shows the correlation between the number of bits and the colours provided:

Bits	Colours
4	16
8	256
16	65536
24	16.777 million
32	About 4300 million

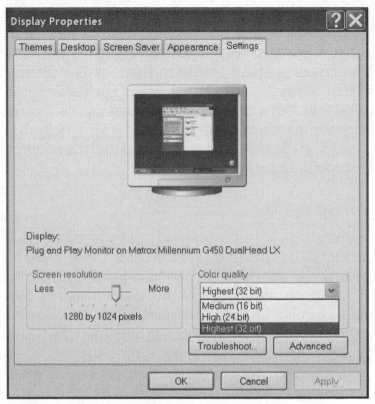

*Fig.4.13 The Color quality menu offers several
colour depths*

In general, higher colour depth settings give better
looking results, especially when photographic images
are displayed. On the other hand, the results obtained
using 16-bit resolution are very good, and there is
probably no point in going beyond 24-bit resolution.
Bear in mind that greater colour depth tends to slow
things down, and that some programs might not

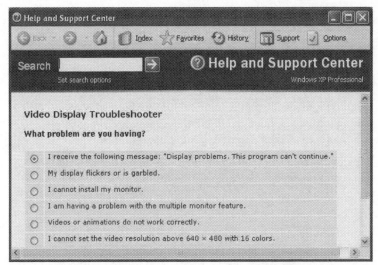

*Fig.4.14 The first page of the Video Display
    Troubleshooter*

operate at a usable speed unless a fairly low colour
depth is used. The optimum colour depth is the lowest
one which gives a display quality that you find
acceptable.

In practice

Having set the required screen resolution and colour
depth, operate the Apply button. It is likely that
Windows is overestimating the abilities of the monitor
if the screen goes blank or produces an unstable
image. The screen should return to normal in a few
seconds though. One way of tackling the problem is
to operate the Troubleshoot button, which launches
the Video Display Troubleshooter (Figure 4.14). By

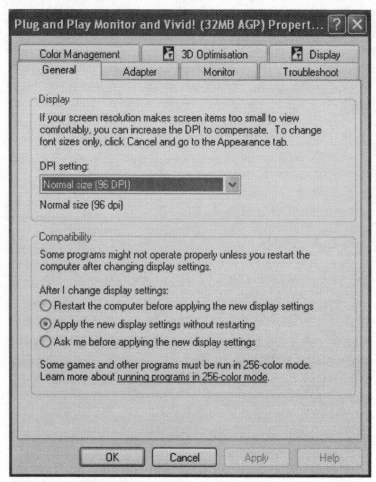

*Fig.4.15 This window gives access to a range of
advanced settings*

going through the questions and suggested cures it
is likely that the problem would soon be solved.
However, the most likely cause of the problem is
Windows setting a scan rate that is too high for the
monitor, and this is easily corrected.

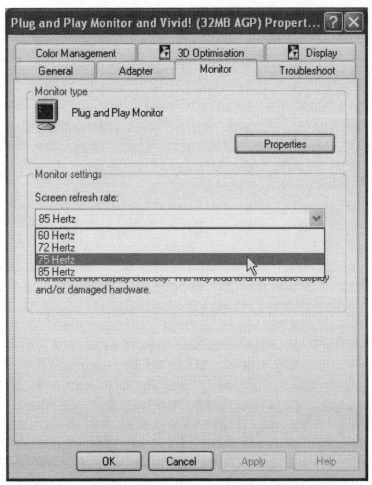

Fig.4.16 Reducing the scan rate slightly should cure the problem

First set the required screen resolution again, and then left-click the Advanced button to bring up a window like the one in Figure 4.15. Next, operate the Monitor tab to switch the window to one like Figure

4.16.   Activate the Screen refresh rate menu, and choose a lower rate than the one currently in use. In this example the rate was reduced from 85 hertz to 75 hertz. Left-click the Apply button and observe the screen.

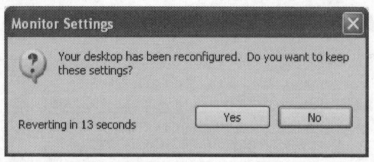

Fig.4.17 If this window appears, left-click the Yes button to keep the new settings

With luck, this time a small window like the one shown in Figure 4.17 will be visible on the screen. If so, operate the Yes button to keep the new scan rate. If not, wait for a proper display to return and then repeat this process using an even lower scan rate. Note that the maximum scan rate for a monitor generally reduces as the screen resolution is increased. Consequently, the higher the screen resolution used, the lower the scan rate that will have to be set.

Language problems

Back in the days of MS-DOS it was often quite tricky to persuade the operating system that you were using a keyboard having the English version of the English

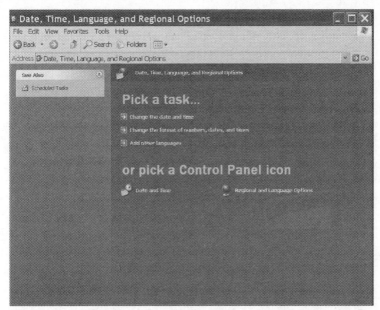

Fig.4.18 Left-click the Date, Time, Language, and Regional Options link

layout, rather than one having the US English characters and layout. The differences are quite minor, but they result in the double quotes and @ symbol being transposed. Also, the pound sign (£) tends to disappear or be replaced with the hash (#) symbol. Some of the little-used symbols also disappear or become assigned to the wrong keys.

It is not unknown for Windows XP to suffer from a similar problem after installation, or when it has been reinstalled. The Windows Control Panel has a keyboard section, which is normally the first place to go if there is a keyboard problem. This is certainly the first place to go if the keyboard is not working at

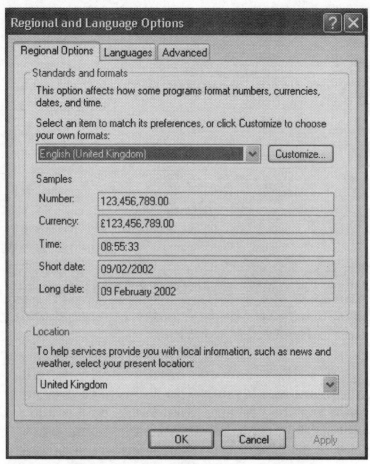

*Fig.4.19 Make sure that English and United
Kingdom are selected in the menus*

all, or if it behaves very erratically. However, with a
language problem it is unlikely to be of any help.

It is better to start by going to the Control Panel and
left-clicking the Date, Time, Language, and Regional
Options link. This switches the Control Panel window

to the one of Figure 4.18, where the Regional and Language icon should be left-clicked. This produces a properties window like the one in Figure 4.19. Make sure that the menu near the top of the window is set to English (United Kingdom). United Kingdom should be selected in the Location menu near the bottom of the window. Where necessary, correct these settings. Operate the Apply and OK buttons to close this window.

To check that everything is correct, look at the bottom right-hand corner of the Windows desktop. Here there will be a button that indicates the language in use. This will usually be marked EN for English, but more than one version of the language will probably be available. Left-click the button to produce a small popup menu (Figure 4.20), and then select the English (United Kingdom) option. The keyboard should then function properly, producing the pound sign, etc. However, the wrong version of English will still be set as the default.

To correct this, activate the menu again and select the Show the language bar option. This removes the button and produces a small floating bar instead (Figure 4.21). Operate the tiny button in the bottom right-hand

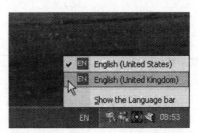

Fig.4.20 The small pop-up menu

corner of the bar and select Settings from the popup menu. This launches the Text Services and Input Languages window (Figure 4.22). Use the pop down menu near the top of the window to select the correct default language. Next operate the Apply and OK buttons, and then restart

Fig.4.21 Select Settings from this menu

the computer to check that the default has switched to the right language.

User accounts

At least one user account is produced when Windows XP is installed. There will often be two accounts, which are the Administrator account, and one for the user of the PC. Both accounts are normally assigned the same password. The idea is for the Administrator account to be used by the person that looks after the computers in an office. Each user of a PC has a separate account, with Windows set up the way that each user likes it when they use their account. As far as possible, each user effectively has their own PC, but obviously only one user at a time can login and utilise each PC.

Some computer retailers supply their PCs fully set up and ready for use, sometimes complete with

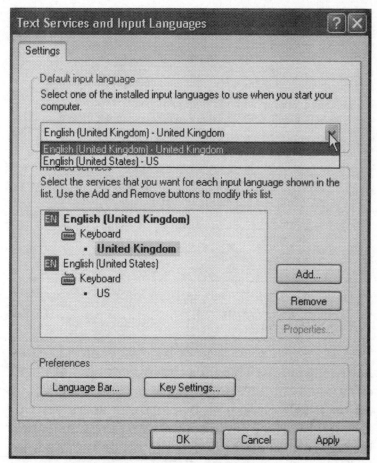

*Fig.4.22 The Text Services and Input Languages
window*

several user accounts installed. However, things do
not normally operate this way if you buy an "off the
shelf" PC, although it is often offered as a fairly pricey
option. Any additional accounts you require normally
have to be set up manually yourself.

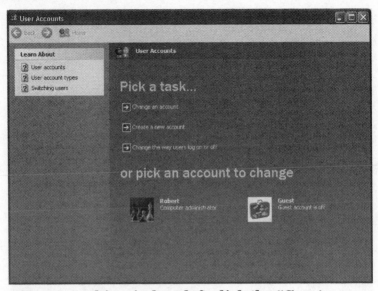

Fig.4.23 At this window, left-click the "Create a new account" link

Of course, user accounts can be irrelevant, especially in a home or small business environment. They may offer no advantages when there is only a single user for each PC. Even with two or three users per PC, they might prefer not to bother with the complication of separate accounts. On the other hand, some individual users do actually have several accounts, with Windows set up in a different fashion for each type of use. It is really a matter of personal preference.

Administrator

The Administrator account is usually reserved for making changes to the system or troubleshooting,

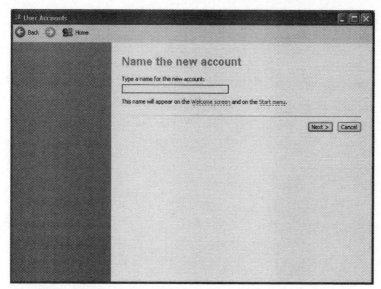

Fig.4.24 Type the name for the new account into the textbox

since it gives full control over the system. As a minimum, there should be at least one additional account for normal use. As pointed out previously, this will often be installed by default. It might be necessary to add it yourself, and you will probably wish to add one or two extra accounts if the PC is for family use.

The first step in adding a new account is to go to the Control Panel and left-click the User Accounts icon or link text. This launches a window like the one in Figure 4.23. Left-click the link for "Create a new account", which switches the window to the one shown in Figure 4.24. Type a name for the account into the textbox and then operate the Next button.

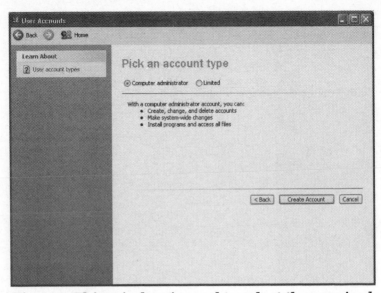

*Fig.4.25 This window is used to select the required
type of account*

The type of account is selected at the next window
(Figure 4.25). An administrator account provides
freedom to make changes to the system, but these
abilities are not needed for day to day use of the
computer. A limited account is generally considered
to be the better choice for normal use, since the
restrictions reduce the risk of the system being
accidentally damaged.

There are a few points to bear in mind if you opt for a
limited account. You might not be able to install
programs when using this type of account. Any that
you do install might not be fully available to other
users. Also, some programs produced prior to

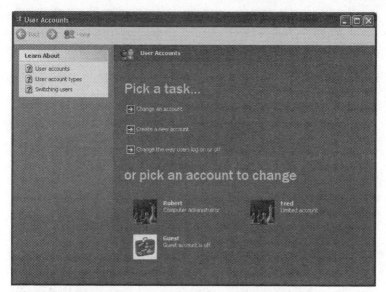

*Fig.4.26 The new account has been added
(compare this with Fig.4.23)*

Windows 2000 and XP might not be usable with a
limited account. It is possible to make changes to
the system that will only affect the limited account,
but any wider ranging changes are likely to be
blocked. It might not be possible to undertake
something as basic as uninstalling a program when
using this type of account. Consequently, there is no
alternative to an administrator account if maximum
flexibility is required.

Having selected the type of account using the radio
buttons, operate the Create Account button. The
original User Accounts window then returns, but it
should now contain the newly created account (Figure

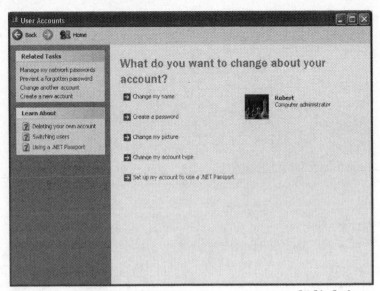

Fig.4.27 Activate the "Create a password" link in the list of tasks

4.26). There are other facilities in the User Accounts window that enable the login and logoff settings to be altered. By default, the Welcome screen is shown at start-up, and you simply have to left-click the entry for the new account in order to use it. Note that the new account will start with a largely blank desktop. Each account has its own desktop and other settings, so each account can be customised with the best settings for its particular user.

Accounts are not password protected by default. To add a password, go to the User Accounts window and left-click the entry for the account that you wish to password protect. This switches the window to look

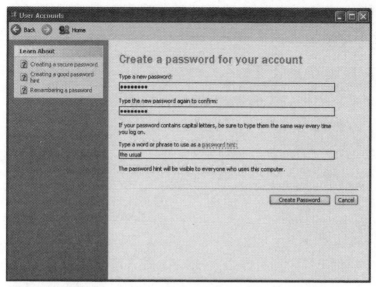

Fig.4.28 The password is entered in the top and middle textboxes

like Figure 4.27, and here the Create password link is activated. At the next window (Figure 4.28) the password is typed into the top two textboxes, and a hint is entered into the other textbox. The hint is something that will jog your memory if you should happen to forget the password.

Next operate the Create Password button, which moves things on to the window of Figure 4.29. This window explains that password protection does not prevent other users from reading your files. Operate the Yes Make Private button if you would like to prevent other users from accessing your files. This completes the process, and the password will be needed the next time you login to that account.

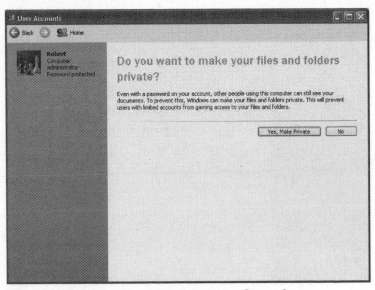

Fig.4.29 You can opt to prevent others from accessing your files

Firewall

The version of Windows supplied with modern PCs is Windows XP Service Pack 2 (SP2). Windows XP SP2 is a major rewrite of the original operating system, and the modifications were mainly aimed at improving security. Security is now a major issue for PC users, especially those that use the Internet. This probably means the vast majority of PC users. The subject of PC security is too vast to be considered in detail here, but it is fully explained in BP540, Easy PC Security and Safety, from the same publisher and author as this book.

The increased security of Windows XP SP2 can provide a few problems for those who are not familiar with the new features. There is a firewall program built into the original version of Windows XP, but it is not activated by default. A rather more advanced firewall program is installed as part of SP2, and it is switched on by default. A firewall is a program or some computer hardware that tries to prevent hackers from gaining access to your PC via a network, such as an Internet connection.

The Windows XP firewall program can confuse users, as it sometimes causes warning messages to appear on the screen when programs are run. This occurs when a program tries to access the Internet and its activity is detected by the firewall. In most cases the program will be something like a media player or web browser that is quite legitimately trying to use the Internet connection.

When asked if you would like to go on blocking the program's Internet access or unblock it, choose to remove the blocking only if you are sure that the program is one that you are using, and that it has good reason to use the Internet connection. Backdoor Trojans, spyware, etc., gather information from a PC and try to send it to hackers via the Internet. The built-in firewall should detect and block most programs of this type provided you do not override it.

There is a potential problem in cases where the computer is equipped with a software firewall other than the built-in program. Security programs, including firewall software, are often bundled with

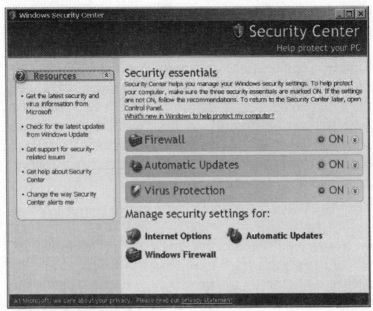

*Fig.4.30 The Security is a new feature of Windows
        XP SP2*

new PCs. In theory it is possible to have two firewall
programs running at the same time, but in practice
it might cause problems. It is probably pointless to
use two firewall programs, since they provide the
same function. Two firewalls will drain the
computer's resources more than using just one, but
little additional protection will be provided. In fact it
is unlikely that any additional protection will be
provided.

The new Windows XP firewall is better than the
original, but it is not as good as most third-party
firewall programs. Consequently, if you have an

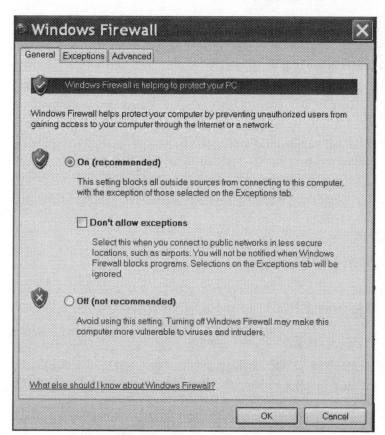

Fig.4.31 The lower radio button enables the built-in firewall to be switched off

alternative firewall program, in most cases it will be best if this is used and the built-in program is switched off. The built-in firewall will probably not offer any facility that is not available from the third-party alternative.

The SP2 update adds a new feature called the Security Center, and this can be accessed via the appropriate icon and link-text in the Windows Control Panel. At the bottom of the Security Center's window (Figure 4.30) there is a Windows Firewall link, and left-clicking this produces a new window (Figure 4.31). The radio button near the bottom of this window enables the firewall to be switched off. Note that it is definitely not a good idea to do this unless an alternative firewall program has been installed, or the PC is not used on any form of network. Operate the OK button to exit the Windows Firewall window and make the changes take effect.

Antivirus

There are two main problems that occur when using Windows XP SP2 with antivirus software. One is that a few of these programs do not do things using the approved methods, which can result in Windows "thinking" that the antivirus software is attacking rather than protecting the system. It is likely that the only way around this problem will be to obtain an updated version of the program or to switch to different antivirus software. Software patches should be available for any major antivirus programs that have this problem, or the manufacturer's web site might give details of a way around the problem. It is unlikely that this problem will occur provided an up-to-date antivirus program is used.

A more common problem is that of the antivirus software not being recognised by the Security Center feature. It is important to realise that although the

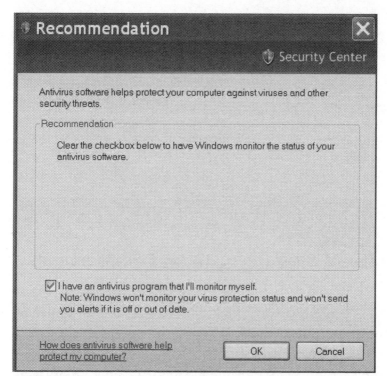

*Fig.4.32 You can opt out of having Windows
monitor the antivirus software*

antivirus software appears to be non-operational, in
the vast majority of cases it will still be working
normally. The problem is simply that the Security
Center has failed to detect and link to the antivirus
program. Most antivirus programs try to protect
themselves from harmful programs such as viruses,
and this can result in them blocking Window's
attempts at detection. This should not really happen
provided you use an up-to-date antivirus program, so

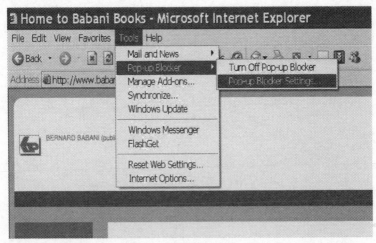

Fig.4.33 Select Pop-up Blocker from the submenu

it is probably worth looking for an update or upgrade
if this problem does occur.

With lesser known antivirus software the problem can
simply be that Windows does not recognise that
particular program. You can opt to monitor the
antivirus program yourself, or rely on the program's
own monitoring and automatic updating facility. A
Recommendations button will appear in the Security
Center if Windows has difficulty monitoring the
antivirus software. Operating this button produces
the Recommendations window.

The checkbox near the bottom of this window must
be ticked (Figure 4.32) if you will monitor the antivirus
software yourself, or rely on its own updating facility.
In theory this should prevent Windows producing a
start-up warning message about no antivirus

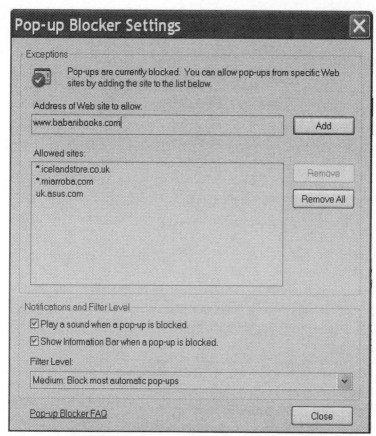

Fig.4.34 The URL (web address) is typed into the textbox near the top of the Window. Operating the Add button then adds it to the list

software being detected. In practice this message might still appear. Using antivirus software that Windows recognises seems to be the only certain way of suppressing this warning.

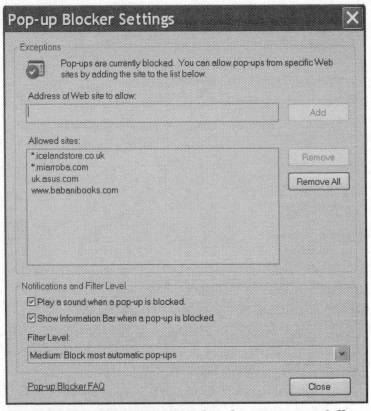

*Fig.4.35 Here the new URL has been successfully
added to the list*

Pop-up blocker

Windows XP SP2 adds a pop-up blocker to Internet
Explorer, and it seems to be very effective. In fact it
can be too effective, causing it to block some features
such as automatic updating facilities or the clever
features offered by some web sites. Blocking can be

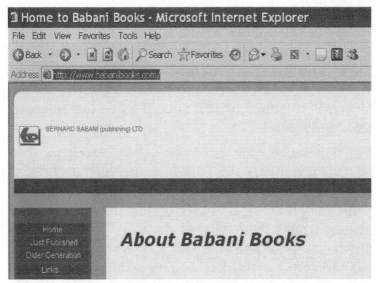

Fig.4.36 Left-clicking on the Address textbox has selected the URL

switched off of course, but a better solution is to enable pop-ups when using the relevant web addresses.

From within Internet Explorer, select Pop-up Blocker from the Tools menu, followed by Pop-up Blocker Settings from submenu that appears (Figure 4.33). Type the URL (web address) into the textbox near the top of the new window that appears (Figure 4.34) and then operate the Add button. The URL should then be added to the "Allowed sites" list in the middle part of the window (Figure 4.35).

Note that you can easily copy a URL from a browser and insert it in a textbox using the Windows Copy and Paste facilities. The normal way of selecting text is to drag the text pointer through it. In other words, you place the pointer at one end of the text you wish to select, press down the left mouse button, and move the pointer to the other end of the block of text while still holding down the mouse button. Then the mouse button is released, which should leave the selected text highlighted.

The normal way for text to be highlighted is for it to be shown in inverse video, which means that the text and background colours are swapped. This makes it stand out clearly from other text so that you can see exactly what is, and what is not, selected. Most web browsers, including Internet Explorer, make it very easy to select a full URL. The whole thing will be selected and highlighted if you simply left-click on any part of the Address textbox (Figure 4.36).

In order to copy text to the Windows Clipboard it is merely necessary to select Copy from the Edit menu (Figure 4.37). An alternative way of copying selected material to the Clipboard is the Control-C method. In other words, press the Control key and the C key while still holding down the Control key. To paste the text into a textbox, left-click within the textbox to ensure it is active, and then select the Paste option from the Edit menu.

With small windows, including the Pop-up Blocker Settings window, there are usually no standard menus such as File and Edit. In such cases, selecting Paste from the Edit menu is obviously not an option. However, the keyboard shortcuts should still work. The keyboard shortcut for the Paste facility is Control-

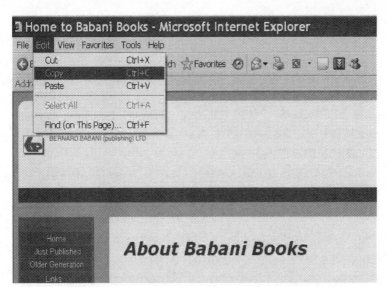

*Fig.4.37 The Copy facility is used to copy the
selected text to the Windows Clipboard*

V. Most of the keyboard shortcuts are probably not
particularly useful for the majority of PC users, but
Control-C and Control-V are two that are well worth
remembering. Control-X (Cut) can also be useful. It
differs from the Copy command in that it copies the
selected material to the Clipboard in the usual way,
but it also deletes the source material.

Points to remember

It is not necessary to register Windows XP in order to use it, but it will stop working after 30 days unless it is activated. Reactivation will be needed if it is reinstalled, and might also be necessary if large changes are made to the hardware. Activation via the Internet is much easier than using the telephone method.

The "bundled" versions of Windows supplied with PCs do not necessarily require product activation. Instead, the supplied copy of Windows is "tied" to that particular PC. Upgrading a bundled version of Windows to a newer type at some time in the future might not be possible. A major hardware upgrade could require a new copy of Windows to be obtained.

The Text Services and Input Languages window can be used to correct things if the computer defaults to using the US English keyboard layout.

By default there will be an Administrator account, and probably one ordinary user account as well. Any others you require must be added by going to the User Accounts window, which is accessed via the Control Panel.

In order to make most changes to the system it is necessary to use the Administrator account, or an account that has administrator privileges. It is generally considered safer if most user accounts do not have Administrator privileges, since this reduces the risk of users making inadvertent changes to the system.

The built-in Windows firewall is switched on by default when using Windows XP SP2. A warning message will be produced the first time practically any program tries to access the Internet. Only give permission for the program to access the Internet if you are sure that it does not represent a security hazard.

The version of Internet Explorer supplied as part of Windows XP SP2 includes a pop-up blocker. This is very efficient at blocking unwanted pop-up advertisements, but it can sometimes prevent web pages from being displayed properly. The best solution for pages that you will visit regularly, is to enable pop-ups for that particular web address.

4 Windows problems

Solving file difficulties

Displaying files

Windows has built-in facilities for displaying several common types of file. For example, if you use Windows Explorer to locate an image file, simply double-clicking its entry will result in the image being displayed. An image file is one that is used to store any form of image, which in modern computing usually means a photograph. However, there are other image types, such as diagrams and technical drawings. Computers are used in a wide variety of applications, and the range of files types used with PCs reflects this diversity.

In Figure 5.1 I have double-clicked on the entry for a photograph in the popular Jpeg format, and Windows Explorer has duly displayed it in a new window. Note that this will only work if the image file is in one of the popular file formats such as Jpeg or GIF. The built-in facilities of Windows will not be able to display an image if you double-click the entry for a file that Windows considers to be an "unknown" file type. Fortunately, the number of image file types in common use has dwindled over recent years, so there

Fig.5.1 Windows has a built-in viewer that can handle Jpeg images

is a good chance of success unless you are dealing with a file from the dim and distant past.

The row of buttons beneath the displayed image provide some control over the way the image is displayed, together with some other facilities such as one that enables the image file to be copied to disc, and another that can be used to print the image. The Print function obviously requires the computer to be equipped with a suitable printer, but these days even the most basic of inkjet printers can handle photographs and other images.

*Fig.5.2 There are some basic facilities, including
the ability to zoom in on part of an image*

If the orientation of the image is wrong, it can be
rotated through 90 degrees using the Rotate button.
The Zoom facility is useful, and it enables part of the
image to be viewed in detail (Figure 5.2). It is possible
to pan around the image using the usual Windows
scrollbars, although this facility often seems to work
quite slowly when viewing high-resolution images.

Windows Explorer usually has icons to represent the
files on a disc, but for image files it might default to
using "thumbnails". A thumbnail in this context is
simply a much smaller version of the full image.

Although a thumbnail image is very small, it usually enables the user to quickly and easily locate the required files. Of course, it could be difficult to tell one image from the next if there are several similar images on offer. Consequently, it might occasionally be necessary to display the full images, one-by-one, until you find the one you are looking for.

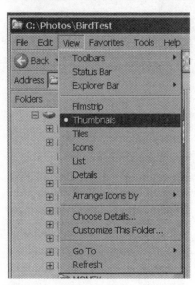

Fig.5.3 Select Thumbnails from the menu

Another potential problem is that it can take Windows a while to generate the thumbnail images, especially where there are large numbers of images in each folder. However, it should only go through this process the first time a folder is viewed. The thumbnails are stored on the disc and are ready for immediate use on any subsequent occasions when the folder is viewed. Despite one or two potential shortcomings, in general it is well worthwhile having the thumbnail images displayed.

If these images are not shown by default, go to the View menu in Windows Explorer and select the Thumbnails option (Figure 5.3). The icons or text entries should then be replaced by the thumbnail

Fig.5.4 Thumbnails are now shown instead of the icons that were used previously

images, as in Figure 5.4. Note that the View option can be set separately for each folder, so you can set the most appropriate mode for each one.

Extensions

If you go into Windows Explorer and double-click the entry for any data file, Windows will try to display the file. In addition to the popular types of image file, Windows will use its built-in facilities to display simple text files. These are also known as "txt" files, because text files often have "txt" as the filename's extension. An extension is typically three or four letters at the

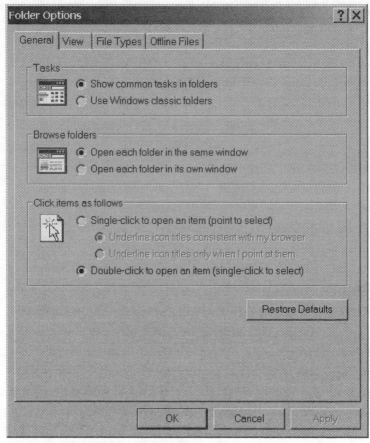

Fig.5.5 The Folder Options window, where the View tab is selected

end of a file's name that indicate its purpose (program, image, text document, or whatever). A full stop is used to separate the extension from the main filename. For example, a file called "document1.doc" is called "document1" and has "doc" as the extension.

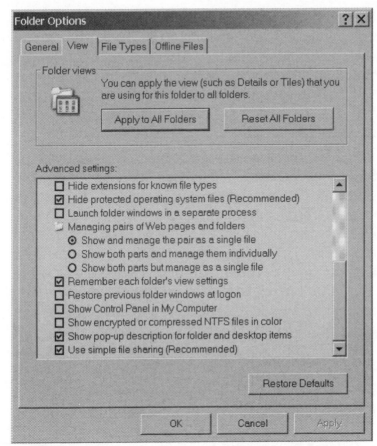

Fig.5.6 A lot of options are available in the View section of the Folder Options window

By default, Windows does not show the extensions of filenames. The icons for files attempt to give you an indication of the file type, but many icons fail to make this totally clear. The extensions for some file types are shown when using the List and Details settings in the View menu of Windows Explorer.

It is possible to force the program to show all file extensions by first going to the Tools menu and selecting Folder Options. This launches the Folder Options window (Figure 5.5), where the View tab is selected. A new version of the window then appears, and this has a long list of settings that are selected using numerous check boxes and radio buttons.

In the list there is an entry called "Hide extensions for known file types". This has been scrolled to the top of the displayed entries in Figure 5.6. In order to disable this function and display the extensions for all file types, left-click the checkbox just to the left of this entry. The tick will disappear from the checkbox to show that this option is no longer selected. Operate the OK button to exit the Folder Options window. The extensions should then be shown when using the List and Details views in Windows Explorer. Figure 5.7 shows the contents of a folder displayed using the List option, and the "jpg" extension of the files indicates that they contain Jpeg images.

Extensions probably seem of little importance to someone making a start in computing. They will certainly be of greater importance after some years of computing, when various types of data file have accumulated on the PC's hard disc. Extensions enable the user to see at once what type of data file they are dealing with, and whether the file is actually a data type at all. Extensions are also essential to the operating system, and they determine how Windows treats files that you try to open.

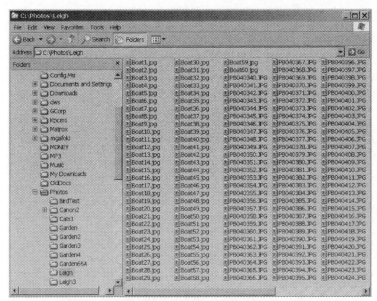

Fig.5.7 Here the contents of a folder are shown using the List option

The treatment of some file types is built into the operating system. For example, files that have an "exe" (executable) or "com" (command) extension are programs, and double-clicking their entries in Windows Explorer will result in them being run. Windows also knows how to deal with popular forms of data file such as Jpeg images and simple text files, but what happens if you double-click an entry for something other than a "run of the mill" data file?

Non-standard files

There are two possible outcomes if you try to open a file that is not one of the standard types that Windows

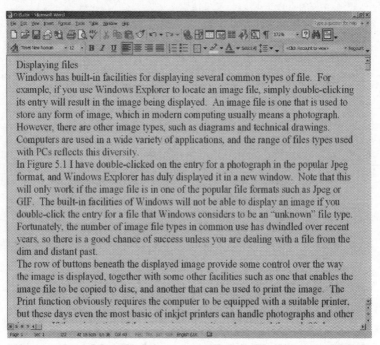

Fig.5.8 Double-clicking on a DOC file has resulted in it being loaded into Microsoft Word

automatically knows how to deal with. With luck, Windows will first run the relevant application program, and then it will load the data file into that program. In Figure 5.8 I have double-clicked on the entry for a file that has a "doc" extension. This is the extension used for documents produced using Microsoft's popular Word program. Word is installed on my PC, so the program has been run and the appropriate file has then been opened.

Windows provides an easy means of opening any files that you have been using recently. Depending on the

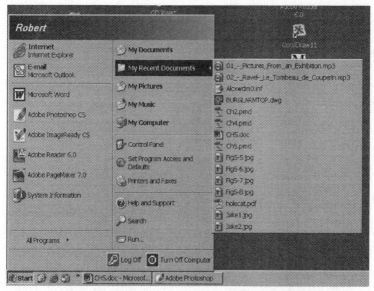

Fig.5.9 My Recent Documents shows the last 15 documents that have been opened

version of Windows in use and how it is set up, there will be an option in the Start menu called either Documents or My Recent Documents. Placing the pointer over this option produces a pop-out menu showing the last 15 files that have been opened (Figure 5.9). Left-clicking the entry for a file will result in it being opened. Where necessary the appropriate application program will also be opened.

File association

Obviously there has to be some mechanism that enables Windows to run the right program when you double-click a data file, and this is handled by the file association facility. This is basically just a list of file types that Windows stores on the hard disc drive, and for each entry there is a corresponding program. When you double-click on a file, Windows refers to this list if the extension is not one that can be handled by its integral facilities. It then runs the corresponding program and opens the file that you activated.

This system should always work properly provided the file is one that originated on your PC. When you install a new program on your PC, where appropriate it will add its data type or types to the list of file type associations. Windows will then know what to do if you activate a file that was produced by that program, or any file of the same type. This system works quite well, but I suppose it is inevitable that problems occur from time to time.

Probably the most common problem is that you double-click a file and it does indeed open, but in the wrong program! In most cases the file is opened using a program that can handle the file type in question, rather than just causing the program to produce an error message when it is unable to load the file.

The usual cause of this problem is that the original file association has been hijacked by a program that you have subsequently installed on your PC. The new program has made itself the default program for that particular type of file, and it has deleted the original association for that file type. Alternatively, a badly written installation program might have accidentally obliterated or altered some of the file associations.

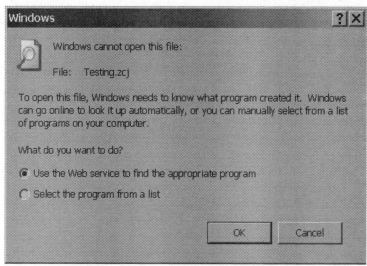

*Fig.5.10 Windows responds with this screen if no
suitable file association is found*

No program

Another common problem is when double-clicking the
entry for a data file does not result in a program being
launched. Instead, Windows produces the response
shown in Figure 5.10. There are two options here,
and the default option is to let Windows search
databases on the Internet in an effort to find the
correct program for the file you are trying to open.

Note that this option requires an active Internet
connection. There is no problem here if you have a
broadband connection that is always active. You just
operate the OK button and wait for a response from
Windows. With a dial-up connection that is not
switched on, you must log on before operating the OK
button.

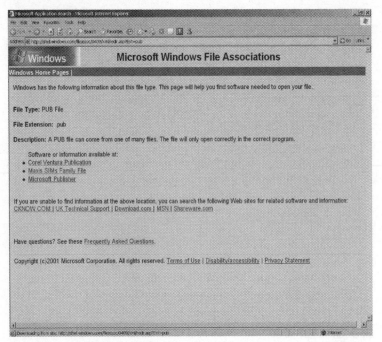

Fig.5.11 Windows has found three programs that use files with a PUB extension

If you are in luck, Windows will find the appropriate program in its database. Some file extensions are used by more than one program, so it is possible that a small list of programs will be provided. This has happened in the example of Figure 5.11, where Windows has found three programs that use a "pub" extension on their data files.

You have to use a little common sense when dealing with this type of thing. The file giving the problem in this case contained a newspaper cutting, and it was likely to be some form of desktop publishing (DTP)

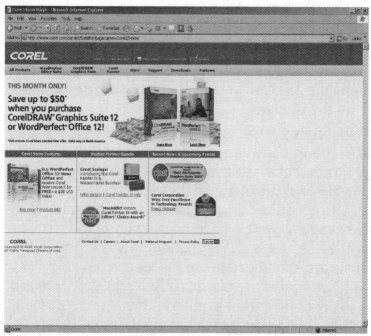

Fig.5.12 This web page shows that Ventura is a product of the Corel Corporation

file. The Ventura and Publisher programs pointed to by Windows are both of the desktop publishing variety. Fortunately, Publisher came as part of the Microsoft Office Suite that was installed on my other PC, and trying the file on that PC resulted in Publisher being launched and the file loading correctly.

Being realistic about things, in most cases you will not have the correct program, and will have to follow the links provided by Windows. Left-clicking the Ventura link in the example of Figure 5.11 moved things on to the web page of Figure 5.12. This shows that Ventura is produced by Corel, the well-known software company. Further investigation shows that it is an expensive program, and not the type of thing you are likely to buy in order to open a file that someone has sent you, or that has been downloaded from the Internet.

Sometimes you will be in luck and there will be a quick and cheap solution. Some files require a reader program that is available as a free download. Having downloaded and installed the program you should be able to open the file and examine its contents. Most file readers permit hard copy to be made via your printer. In most cases though, it is not possible to make any modifications to the loaded data file. This usually requires a piece of commercial software that is likely to be quite expensive. If someone has sent you a file or you have downloaded one from the Internet, there is a good chance that viewing the file and printing it will be the only facilities that you require.

Note that there is no guarantee that Windows will be able to locate the program needed to open a data file. If the file is used with an obscure program it is likely that a screen like the one shown in Figure 5.13 will be produced. This gives a link to an online database of file extensions, plus one or two other suggestions. However, probably your best bet is to seek clarification from whoever supplied you with the file. Having generated the file, they should be able to give guidance on how to open it.

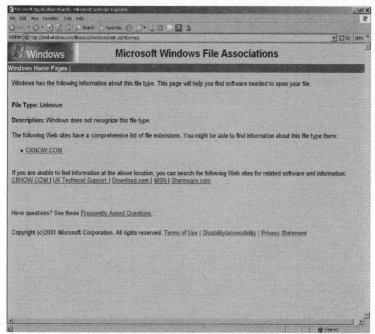

Fig.5.13 This page provides a link to an online database of file extensions

Associations list

You can obtain a list of the file associations by going to the Windows Control Panel and double-clicking the Folder Options icon. With some versions of Windows this is the Files and Folders icon, or something similar. A new window will be launched (Figure 5.14), and the next step is to operate the Files tab near the top of the window.

This changes the window, and in the upper section it will show a scrollable list of the associated file types. Left-clicking an entry in the list will highlight it, and

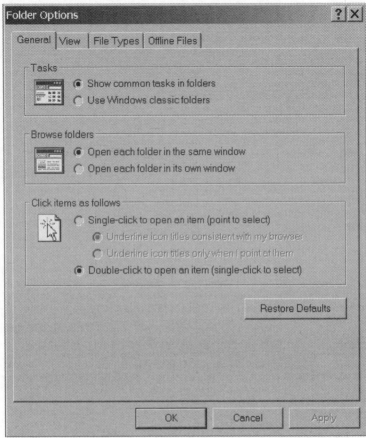

Fig.5.14 Operate the Files tab near the top of this window

the program associated with it will then be named in the lower part of the window. In the example of Figure 5.15, the "JPG" entry has been highlighted, and the lower part of the window indicates that this is associated with the Windows Picture and Fax Viewer

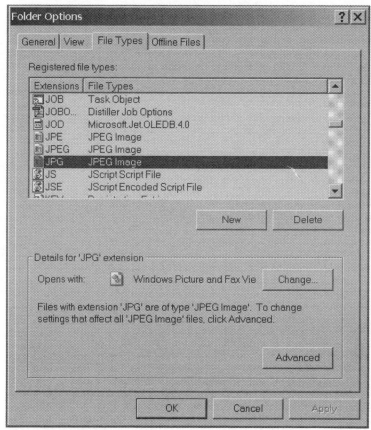

Fig.5.15 JPG files are associated with the built-in Picture and Fax Viewer program

program. This is one of the built-in programs of Windows.

If an association is not as required, it can be changed by highlighting the appropriate entry in the list and operating the Change button. A new window is then

5 Solving file difficulties

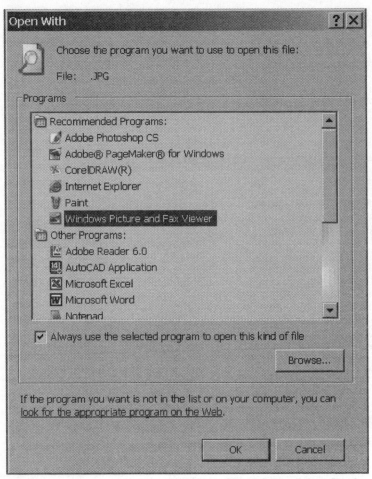

Fig.5.16 This window shows a list of the installed programs

launched, and this shows a list of the installed programs (Figure 5.16). Left-click the correct program to select it, and then operate the OK button to close the window. In this example the "JPG"

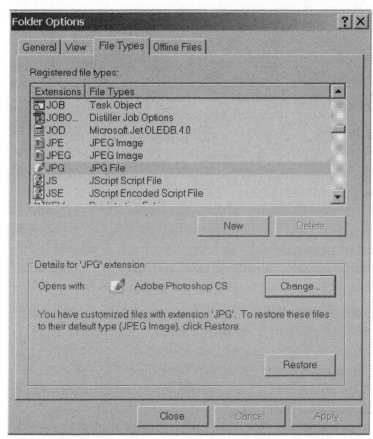

Fig.5.17 Files having a JPG extension are now associated with the correct program

extension had become associated with the built-in file viewer instead of the Photoshop CS program. I therefore selected the Photoshop CS entry, operated the OK button, and back in the Folder Options window the correct association had been restored (Figure 5.17).

There is a possible complication when changing file associations, and this is caused by some very simple programs not being installed in Windows in the normal way. In most cases these programs are not installed in Windows at all, but due to their basic nature they will still manage to work properly when run. Since these programs are not installed in Windows, they do not appear in the list of installed programs, and there is no easy way to associate a file type with one them. It can be done by operating the Browse button, which launches the standard Windows file browser. This is then used to locate and select the correct program file. This is easy enough for those with plenty of computing experience, but it can not be recommended for beginners.

Fortunately, these days the vast majority of programs are installed in Windows, and this problem is unlikely to occur. Remember that it should be possible to run the appropriate program and then load a data file. Therefore, it is not essential to have a file association in order to open a data file.

Download low-down

These days the Internet is probably the main source of files of a type that can not be handled by a PC's built-in facilities. Sometimes a so-called "plug-in" is needed in order to make a certain facility of a web site operational. The plug-in is an application program that adds facilities to Internet Explorer, which is the built-in web browser of Windows. The

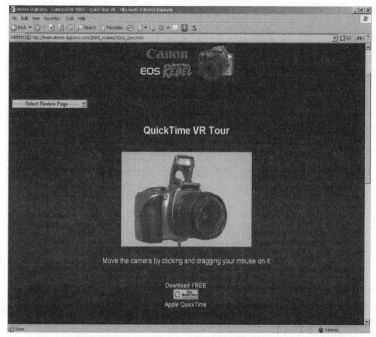

Fig.5.18 The camera can be rotated, but only with the help of Apple QuickTime

most common cause of Internet Explorer needing a plug-in is a web site which has some fancy graphics that require a certain program to be installed. The program is called up by Internet Explorer, and in most cases it runs in the background. To the user it appears as though Internet Explorer is providing the fancy graphics, but they are actually being handled by the plug-in program.

When an additional program is required, it is normal for the web site to indicate that this is the case. In the example of Figure 5.18, by dragging the mouse it

257

is possible to rotate the camera and view it from any angle. This facility is provided by the Apple QuickTime program, and with this particular PC the rotating image is working properly, so QuickTime has obviously been installed previously. However, there is a link to the free QuickTime player program at the bottom of the page, so following this link should soon get the program installed and running.

Another plug-in you are likely to encounter before too long when surfing the Internet is Macromedia's Flash Player. Like QuickTime, this program is often used to provide a web site with movies, interactive graphics, or some other form of interactivity. Many sites that use Flash also offer users a non-Flash version, so you can use the simpler version if preferred. Although the non-Flash site will lack the clever features of the Flash version, it should be a lot quicker in operation. If you have an ordinary dial-up Internet connection it is probably best to opt for the non-Flash version. Some of the pages might otherwise take a long time to load.

Sites that use Flash will sometimes have a link to the download site for the free Flash Player program. However, when surfing the web it is likely that before too long a pop-up message appear, explaining that you need to install the Flash Player before the site will work properly. These days the Flash plug-in may already be installed on the system, but you can still get pop-up messages informing you that a newer version is required.

Either way, the message will provide a link to the download site, or you might simply be asked if you wish to install it. If you give permission for the installation to go ahead, the program or update will probably be installed automatically, with no further intervention being required from the user. Where necessary follow the link and the instructions that are provided.

Security

Unfortunately, the web contains countless sites that try to dupe users into downloading and installing all sorts of malicious programs on their PCs. You therefore have to be very careful about installing any download on your PC. A download could be something perfectly innocent, but it could also be a virus, worm, Trojan, or spyware program. When using the Internet it is advisable not to take anything at face value.

Be especially careful with anything that offers something free if you download and install a program. It used to be free pornography that was used as the lure, but these days it has spread to include various types of software for your PC. Along with the freebie you will probably be installing another program that tries to hijack your PC, produces pop-up advertisements while you are surfing the Internet, or something of this general type. Sometimes there is a warning that more than the freebie will be installed, but it is usually tucked away in the fine print where you are unlikely to notice it.

Unless you really know what you are doing, there is a lot to be said for not allowing any automatic downloads. Distinguishing between safe downloads and those that are not what they seem can be difficult even for those with many years of computing and Internet experience. Staying "ahead of the game" is difficult, with new tricks appearing all the time. Newcomers to computing and the Internet are really just trusting to luck if they permit automatic downloads.

There is a security system that relies on certificates of authenticity. The idea is that the certificate appears on the screen, and that it shows the name of the company that produced the software you are being offered. Although fine in theory, there have been attempts to fake the certificates.

Also, the usefulness of this system is dependent on users knowing that the named company is one that is fully trustworthy. You might download software that is what it is supposed to be, but also contains adware or some other dubious software that was mentioned in the fine print that you never read during the installation process. The software and company are legitimate, but this is of little comfort when pop-advertisements start appearing each time you move to a different web page.

Front door

A simple but effective way of greatly reducing the risk of downloading software is to use the so-called "front

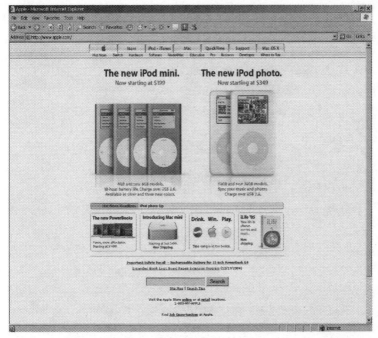

*Fig.5.19 The obvious starting point for the Apple
QuickTime player is the Apple homepage
at www.apple.com*

door" approach. In other words, when offered an
automatic download or a download via a link, you
always opt not to proceed. Instead, you go to the
appropriate web site by typing its web address into
Internet Explorer, or whatever browser program you
are using. You do not have to know the web address,
because there are well-established sites that have
links to all the popular downloads. I suppose that
strictly speaking this is not going in by the front door,
but is instead using a safe side entrance. With both

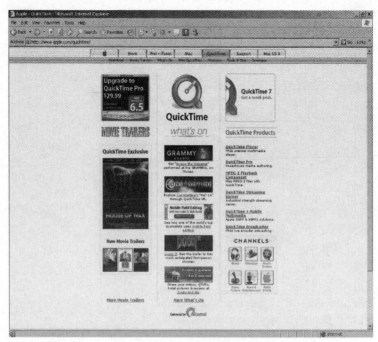

*Fig.5.20 Operating the QuickTime tab on the
          homepage moves things on to this screen*

methods you avoid using what could be a dubious
route that does not lead to the real site.

To try downloading the Apple QuickTime Player via
the front door method I guessed that it would be
somewhere on the www.apple.com site. Typing this
into Internet Explorer's Address textbox produced
the Apple homepage (Figure 5.19), and operating the
QuickTime tab at the top of the page produced the
new page of Figure 5.20. There is a link to the free
QuickTime Player in the QuickTime Products section
down the right-hand side of the page, and operating
this one moves things on to the page of Figure 5.21.

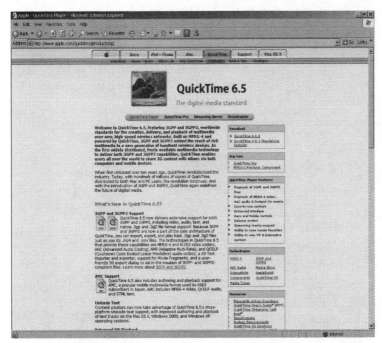

*Fig.5.21 This page provides information about the
QuickTime Player and a download link*

This page provides a great deal of information about
the player, plus the all-important link to the download
page. This is near the top right-hand corner of the
page. Finally, at the next page (Figure 5.22) the initial
stages of downloading the program commence. Note
that it is quite normal for web sites to lead you to free
downloads via rather long routes. Some of the pages
provide useful information about the program you are
about to download, but much of it is advertising that
tries to persuade you to buy a more upmarket version
of the program.

5 Solving file difficulties

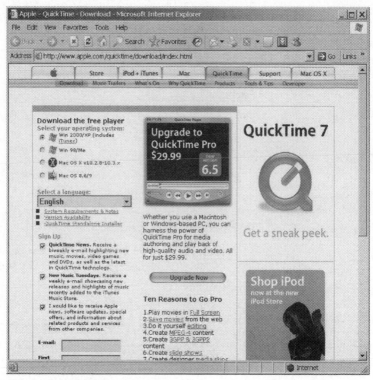

Fig.5.22 At this page you have to select the correct operating system

Once at the page of Figure 5.22 you have to select the correct operating system. Note that most programs for the PC exist in a version for Windows XP plus another version for Windows 98/ME. In this case there are further variants for Mac computers, and with some programs there is also a version for computers that run under Linux. If you are using a new PC it will presumably be the Windows XP edition of the program that is required. The Windows XP radio button is selected by default, so there is no need to make a change here.

Next you have to select a language from the drop-down menu. Most of the popular programs are available in several languages. The selected language is the one that will be used for messages during the installation process, and also on menus, etc., in the program itself.

Opting out

Below this menu there are three checkboxes that are used to opt in or out of regular Emails from Apple on various topics. By all means opt in when this type of thing provides something that is really of interest to you. In most cases though, it is a matter of opting out of everything in order to prevent your Email address from being overrun with numerous newsletters that are really just thinly disguised advertisements.

Further down the page there are textboxes where your name and Email address are added. You can use any name you like if you are unhappy about using your real name. When dealing with large and respected companies it is unlikely that you will receive any Emails from them, apart from any you have opted to receive. With smaller companies I suppose that the risk of receiving unsolicited Emails from them is greater. There is also a greater risk of them passing your Email address to other companies.

A fictitious Email address will usually suffice, but most people take the alternative route of having an Email address specifically for this type of thing. You will probably have to visit the account every now and then in order to keep it open, but there is no need to delete any Emails that are received. You can simply let them accumulate in what is otherwise an unused Email account.

It is easy to obtain a "spare" Email address for this type of thing, and it is just a matter of signing up to one of the free Email services such as Yahoo! or Hotmail. The advantage of this system is that you can obtain freebies even if a real Email address is required. Sometimes a serial number for the program is sent to you via an Email. If you use a fictitious Email address it will not be possible to retrieve the serial number and activate the program. Fortunately, this type of thing seems to be quite rare these days, and it is not a system that is used with the QuickTime Player.

Start downloading

Scrolling down to the bottom of the page reveals the Download button, but this does not start the download. Instead, it moves the process on to the page shown in Figure 5.23. Here, at last, there is a link that does lead to the file for the QuickTime program. In most cases it is merely necessary to left-click the link in order to start the download process, and that was certainly sufficient in this case.

When the left-click method fails, it is worth trying the alternative of right-clicking the link, and then selecting the Save Target As option from the pop-up

*Fig.5.23 At last, the link that leads to the
         QuickTime Player program*

menu. The site probably has a problem if that does
not start the download process. It is then a matter of
trying again later to see if the problem has been fixed.

Storing files

Assuming that everything works correctly, Internet
Explorer will launch the download window, but this
will immediately be covered by a file browser (Figure
5.24). It is up to you where the download is stored on

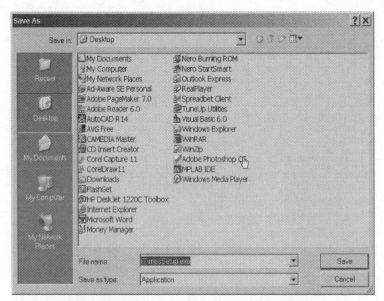

*Fig.5.24 The file browser is use to select the
destination for the downloaded file*

the hard disc, but it is advisable to have a folder
specifically for downloaded files that you intend to
keep. With a program such as QuickTime you might
prefer to delete the file once the program has been
installed.

For people with a broadband connection it is probably
not worthwhile keeping downloads that are unlikely
to be used again, but can be downloaded quickly and
for nothing if they should happen be needed again.
For those with a dial-up connection it is probably best
to keep downloaded files in case they are needed
again. This is definitely the case with files of a few
megabytes or more in size.

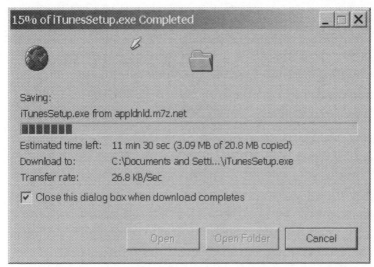

*Fig.5.25 A bargraph shows how well (or otherwise)
the download is progressing*

I decided that the file would be deleted once the
program had been installed, and therefore opted to
download it to the Windows Desktop. One advantage
of using the Desktop is that you can not easily overlook
the file and forget to delete it. It also makes the file
easy to locate and delete once the program has been
installed. Anyway, having pointed the browser to the
location where you would like to store the downloaded
file, operate the Save button.

This will close the file browser and return things to
the download window (Figure 5.25). Windows usually
keeps the user informed about the way any long
process is progressing, and this is no exception. The
window has a bargraph that roughly indicates how

far the download has progressed, and the title bar at the top of the window shows how much of the file has been downloaded in percentage terms. File downloads usually progress very reliably when using a broadband connection, but the same is not always true with dial-up connections.

It might become apparent that things have ground to a halt, and it is then a matter of going back to the download page and trying again. Occasionally a download will continue from where it left off, but in most cases the process starts from scratch. There are programs that are designed to manage downloads more efficiently than the built-in facilities of Internet Explorer. In particular, they permit most broken downloads to be resumed from where they left off. It is probably worthwhile obtaining one of these download managers if you need to download files quite frequently.

Preliminaries

The QuickTime Player is now part of Apple's iTunes program, and at about 22 megabytes it is a substantial download. With a broadband connection it usually possible to download at a few megabytes per minute, but with a dial-up connection the download rate is usually a few minutes per megabyte. A 22 megabyte download is likely to take over an hour, but it should eventually be completed successfully. The download window will automatically close if the checkbox near the bottom left-hand corner is ticked. It will otherwise

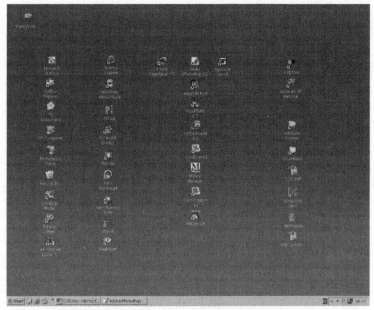

*Fig.5.26 The downloaded file has appeared on the
Desktop in the top left-hand corner*

remain on the screen, and you can run the installation
program by operating the Open button.

The checkbox was ticked on the PC used for this
demonstration, and the download window therefore
closed automatically. In order to run the installation
program it was therefore necessary to locate the
downloaded file and double-click it. As it was
downloaded to the Windows Desktop this was not
difficult. When files are downloaded to the Desktop
they are normally placed in the top left-hand corner,
and the icon for the newly downloaded file was indeed
placed here (Figure 5.26).

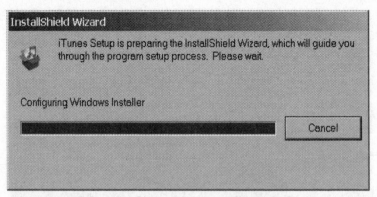

*Fig.5.27 This window appears during the
program's initial setting up period*

When an installation file is opened it is quite normal
for nothing much to happen at first. In this example
the small window of Figure 5.27 is produced, and this
informs the user that the installation program is being
set up. Like any program, the installation program
has to be loaded into memory before it can be run.
This usually takes only a small amount of time though,
and the lengthy delays associated with installation
programs are for different reasons.

Many programs files, but particularly those files that
are downloaded from the Internet, are in a
compressed form. Compressing a file has the
advantage of reducing its size so that there is less to
download. This can greatly reduce the amount of time
taken to complete the download. The program file is
not usable in its compressed form though, and it must
be expanded back to its original state before the
program can be installed.

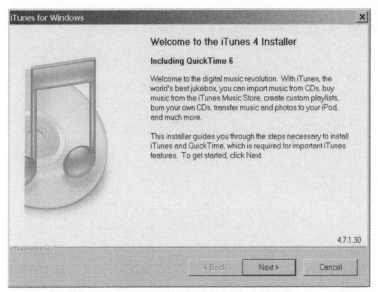

Fig.5.28 This is just an information screen and an advertisement for the iTunes site

Installation programs intended for download normally have the program itself and any support files merged into a single self-extracting archive file. What this means in practice is that you do not need to expand the program file before it can run. As the downloaded program file is run, it automatically expands its contents, goes through the installation process, and then deletes the expanded files as they are no longer needed. Actually, the expanded files are sometimes left on the hard disc, but with the high capacities of modern hard drives this is not of great importance.

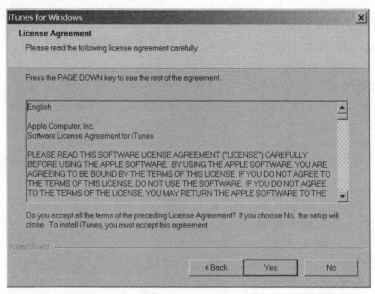

Fig.5.29 When installing practically any program
you have to agree to licensing conditions

Most installation programs will, at an early stage,
check one or two details about your computer and
the software installed on it. This can be necessary
for a variety of reasons. For example, installing a
program for the wrong version of Windows can
seriously damage the Windows installation. Where
appropriate, most installation programs will check
that the operating system of your PC matches the
version of the program that you are trying to install.
The program might check to see if there is an earlier
version already installed. It can sometimes be
necessary to uninstall an old version before a new
one is installed.

Questions, questions

An information screen (Figure 5.28) is produced once the preliminaries are out of the way and the program is ready to proceed with the installation. Operating the Next button moves things on to the inevitable licence agreement (Figure 5.29), and installation can only proceed if you operate the Yes button and agree to the licensing conditions. A screen with some basic information about the iTunes program appears next.

Often, as in this case, it includes the minimum specification needed to run the program. Even if you do not bother to read the rest, it is a good idea to look down this list to see if there is any obvious deficiency in the system you are using. Although some programs will refuse to install on a system that is inappropriate or inadequate in some way, there is no guarantee that this will be the case. It is therefore a good idea to check carefully for anything that is likely to give problems.

Apart from some games, these days there are few programs that require a high specification PC in order to run at all. The usual causes of problems are items of hardware that do not come as standard with a typical PC. For instance, a DVD rewriter or a high specification audio system might be required. In most cases the software will still run if the computer is a bit lacking in certain departments, but some features of the program will be absent or will only operate in a limited fashion.

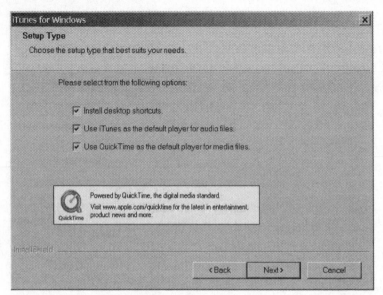

*Fig.5.30 The page gives three options. Opting for a
Desktop icon provides an easy way of
launching the program*

Moving on to the next screen (Figure 5.30), there are
three options on offer. An entry in the Start –
Programs menu is usually added automatically for
any normal program. An icon on the Windows
Desktop and (perhaps) one on the taskbar are
sometimes added automatically, but these days they
are more likely to be optional extras. In this case,
ticking the top checkbox will result in a Desktop icon
being installed. Whether this is a worthwhile addition
is to some extent a matter of personal preference.

In general it is worth having a Desktop icon for
programs that you will use a fair amount, as it

provides a quick and easy means of launching them. It is probably not worthwhile cluttering the Desktop with icons for programs that will be used only rarely, if at all. Note that you can delete an unwanted Desktop icon by right-clicking it and selecting Delete from the pop-up menu. Operate the Yes button when a pop-up message asks if you are sure that you wish to delete the item.

You can produce a Desktop icon for a program by first finding its entry in the Start-Programs menu, and then right-clicking it. From the pop-up menu select Copy, and not as one might have thought, Create Shortcut. Next go to the Windows Desktop and right-click at the point where you would like the icon for the shortcut to appear. Select Paste from the pop-up menu, and the shortcut's icon should be added to the Desktop. Double-clicking the icon should launch the program in the usual, way.

Default program

The remaining two options enable iTunes to be used as the default audio player, and QuickTime to be used as the default program for playing media files. In this case the term "media files" presumably means any files that has some form of video content and not just sound. The choice is yours, but I would be inclined to leave the Windows Media Player as the default program, and only use iTunes and QuickTime for files that are designed specifically for these players.

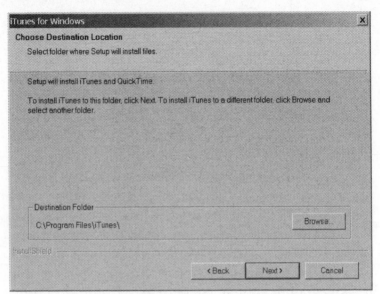

*Fig.5.31 Unless there is a good reason for doing
otherwise, accept the default folder*

Folders

When installing practically any program you are given
the opportunity to change the folder that will be used
to store the program itself and any support files, and
this is no exception (Figure 5.31). With the more
complex programs there can be hundreds or even
thousands of these support files stored in various
subfolders. If you double-click the My Computer icon
on the Windows Desktop, and then double-click the
icon for Drive C (the main hard disc drive), Windows
Explorer will show the contents of the drive. Figure
5.32 shows the contents of drive C on my PC.

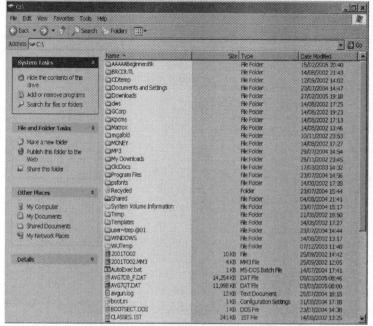

Fig.5.32 Here Windows Explorer is being used to show the contents of drive C on my PC

In days gone by there would have been many more folders, since there would have been one for each program installed on the PC. These days there is a folder called Program Files, and this is present on every PC that operates under a modern version of Windows. This folder is placed there when Windows is installed, and it is the default location for installed programs. It contains a subfolder for each installed program. Initially it will be largely empty, but it will fill up over a period of time. Figure 5.33 shows less than half the folders present in the Program Files

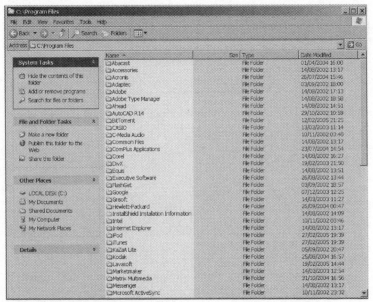

*Fig.5.33 This screen shows less than half the
          subfolders present in the My Programs
          folder*

folder of my PC! Unless there is a good reason for a
program installed elsewhere, just opt to have the
program installed in the default location.

The next screen (Figure 5.34) is just an
advertisement. Operating the Next button starts the
installation process and moves things on to the screen
of Figure 5.35. This has the customary bargraph to
show how things are progressing. It will soon be
replaced by the screen of Figure 5.36, which indicates
that the program has been successfully installed.
Operating the Finish button closes the window and
completes the installation.

Fig.5.34 The first screen is just an advertisement for the iTunes site

Preamble

The main point of this exercise was to install the QuickTime Player program, and this has been achieved. Double-clicking its Desktop icon or selecting its entry from Start-Programs menu had the desired result and ran the player (Figure 5.37). Web pages and CD-ROMs that required the services of the player were also found to work properly. In addition to the QuickTime Player, the iTunes program is installed. Running this proved to be less straightforward, with a certain amount of preamble involved. Unfortunately, this type of thing is increasingly common.

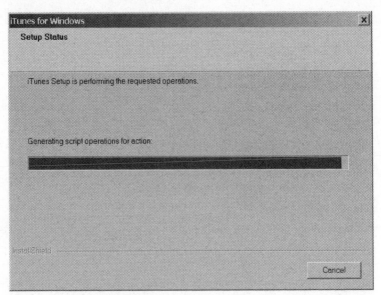

*Fig.5.35 The customary bargraph shows how far
installation has progressed*

First you have to answer Yes to accept the user
agreement, and then the Welcome screen of Figure
5.38 appears. As this explains, it is necessary to
answer some further questions in order to get the
program configured correctly. A certain amount of
configuration by the user is required in order to get a
fair proportion of modern programs "up and
running". This can be necessary to match the
program to the particular hardware you are using, or
simply to get it operating in the way that best suits
your particular requirements.

The installation process tends to have basically the
same steps for each program, but any configuration

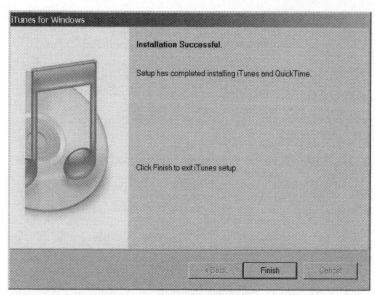

Fig.5.36 The program has been successfully installed

is inevitably different for each piece of software. The type of configuration required, if any, depends on the purpose of the program. In this example we are dealing with a program that is used for playing music, and it handles three types of audio file. Configuring the program ensures that it handles audio files in the way that best suits your requirements. Figure 5.39 shows the first of the configuration screens.

AAC (advanced audio coding) files are in iTunes own format. MP3 is the most popular of the audio file formats, and it is the one that is most familiar to the "man or woman in the street". The iTunes program can play MP3 files. WMA (Windows media audio) is

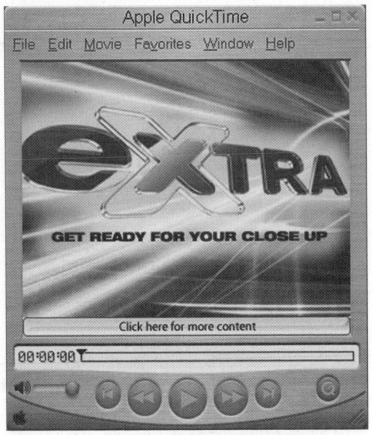

*Fig.5.37 The Apple QuickTime Player has been
installed and runs correctly*

Window's own audio format. While WMA is not as
widely used as MP3, it is still very popular and
preferred by many. Although iTunes can not play
WMA files, it can automatically convert them to AAC
format so that they are effectively made compatible
with this player.

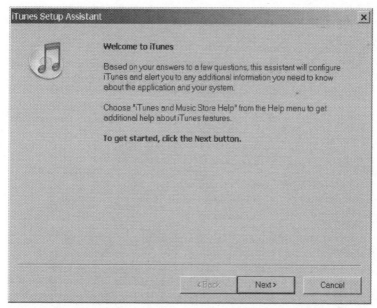

Fig.5.38 The Welcome screen explains that some setting up is required

My Documents

The screen of Figure 5.39 explains this, and also points out that the program can search the My Music folder and add any MP3 or AAC files to your iTunes music library. When Windows is installed it automatically produces a folder called My Documents, and this is used to store your word processor files or other documents.

During installation, Windows also produces four subfolders in the My Documents folder. These are called My eBooks, My Pictures, My Music, and My Videos, and their names make their intended

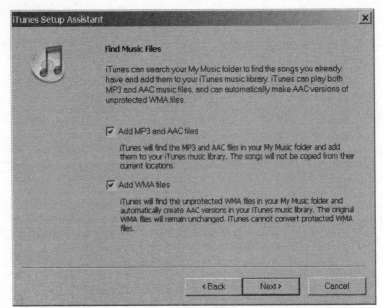

*Fig.5.39 The iTunes program can search for files
to be added to the library*

functions self-evident. If you double-click the My
Computer icon on the desktop, and then the My
Documents link in the window that pops up, you will
see these subfolders listed in the contents of this
folder (Figure 5.40).

Ticking the upper checkbox will result in the iTunes
program searching for AAC and MP3 files, and those
that it finds will be added to the iTunes music library.
Ticking the lower checkbox adds WMA files to the
library, but they are converted into AAC format. Note
that your original WMA files will be left intact and
will not be altered in any way. The new AAC files are

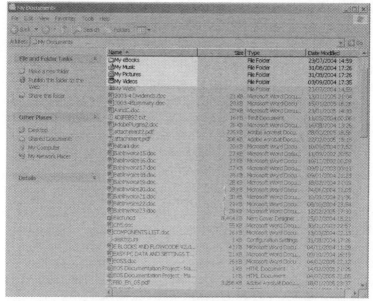

*Fig.5.40 Windows automatically adds these
subfolders during installation*

in addition to the originals and do not replace them.
Of course, this means that some hard disc space will
be consumed by the new files, which could be
significant if you have large numbers of WMA files.

Protected WMA files can not be converted. Music
files that you make yourself, by ripping tracks from a
CD for example, do not usually have any form of copy
protection. Files that are legitimately downloaded
from the Internet are almost certain to have some
form of copy protection. In many cases they can only
be played on the PC that was used to download them.
You can copy the files to another PC, but they will not

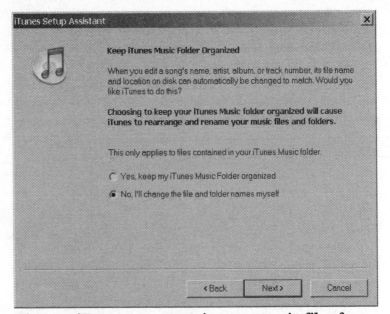

Fig.5.41 iTunes can organise you music files for you, or you can do it yourself

play on any other PC. Conversion to another format is usually blocked as well, so the inability of iTunes to convert protected files is not a shortcoming of the program. It is a general restriction that applies to all media programs.

Operating the Next button moves things on to the window of Figure 5.41. Here you use the radio buttons to either have iTunes organise you music files for you, or to do it yourself. This is a matter of personal preference. Having the program organise things for you looks like the easy way of doing things. However, as a general rule it is better if you do this type of thing yourself. Relying on a program to organise things

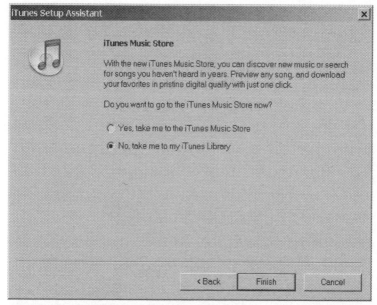

*Fig.5.42 Operating the Finish button completes the
setting up and closes the window*

might work well or you might find that it simply
confuses matters.

The next window (Figure 5.42) is just an
advertisement that invites you to visit the iTunes
online store. Operating the Finish button completes
the setting up, and the program is launched (Figure
5.43). In Figure 5.44 I have added some files to the
program's library and it is playing the first file.

Deleting

Back in the days of the MS/DOS operating system it
was very easy to uninstall a program. You simply

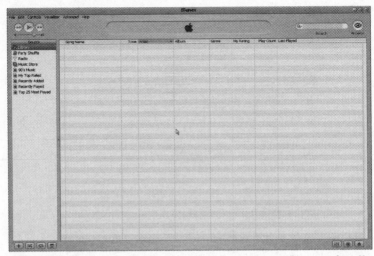

Fig.5.43 The iTunes program is "up and running"

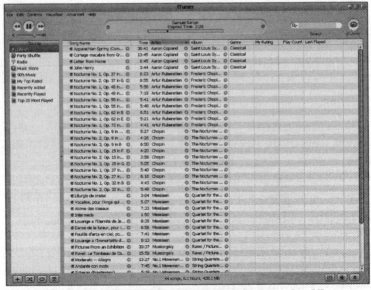

*Fig.5.44 Some files have been added to the library
and one of them is being played*

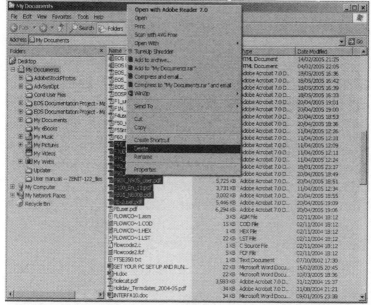

*Fig.5.45 Files or folders can be erased by selecting
them, right-clicking on a selected object,
and then choosing Delete from the menu*

deleted it from the hard disc drive, together with any
files associated with it. New users of Windows have
been known to take a similar approach, and it is
certainly easy to remove unwanted files and folders
using Windows Explorer. You simply select the
objects to be removed, right-click on one of them, and
select the Delete option from the pop-up menu
(Figure 5.45). When asked if you are sure that you
wish to delete the selected objects, operate the Yes
button to go ahead and erase them.

Deleting data files that you have produced using an application program is perfectly safe in the sense that it will not prevent Windows from working properly. It is clearly something that needs to be given due consideration though, and you need to be sure that the files will never be needed again.

If the hard disc drive starts to fill up with files there will be no option but to delete some of them. Windows can only work if it has a reasonably large amount of free disc space to use for storing temporary files. What counts as reasonable depends on the type of programs you will be running, but at least a few hundred megabytes is required.

Files should not be deleted unless you are certain that they will not be needed any more. If some files have to be deleted in order to free space on the hard disc drive, copy them to CDR discs or some other form of mass storage media. Anyway, important files should always be backed up on CDR discs, DVDs, or some other form of external storage.

A serious fault in a hard disc drive could render its contents unreadable. There are data recovery services that can often copy all or most or the data from a damaged hard disc, but there is no guarantee that it will be possible to save any data if your hard drive develops a serious fault. The cost of these services is prohibitively expensive for most non-business users. It is best to work on the basis that any data on the hard disc will be lost if it develops a fault, and that it is just a matter of time before it does develop a fault.

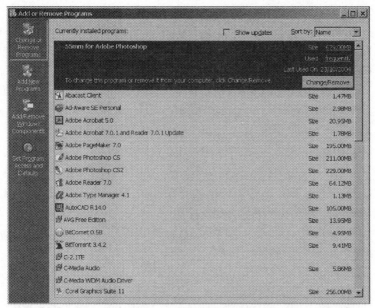

*Fig.5.46 The Windows XP Uninstaller. The exact
appearance depends on the particular
programs that are installed*

Deleting anything other than data files is not
advisable, as it is easy to delete something that is vital
to the normal running of computer. Windows XP is
relatively good at protecting itself from this type of
inexpert deleting, and many of its most important files
are normally hidden from the user. It is still possible
to erase something important though. This could
prevent the PC from booting properly, but it is more
likely to cause irritating error messages during the
boot process. It could also result in some application
programs failing to work properly.

293

If a program is no longer needed and you would like to remove it from the hard disc drive, Windows has a built-in uninstaller that can be accessed from the Control Panel. With the Control Panel in the Classic View, double-click the Add or Remove Programs icon. This produces a window that will look something like Figure 5.46, but its exact appearance will depend on the programs that are installed on your PC.

Removing a program is just a matter of selecting it from the list and then operating the Add/Remove button (Windows ME) or the Change/Remove button (Windows XP). If there are separate Change and Remove buttons, then it is obviously the Change button that is operated. Confirm that you wish to remove the program when prompted in the new window that appears, and the removal process will then begin. The uninstaller should know what can be removed safely, and should only remove files that will not be needed once the program has been uninstalled.

Points to remember

Windows has some built-in facilities for displaying text and graphics files. Trying to open more exotic types of file will result in the appropriate program being opened and the file being loaded into the program. Of course, this system will only work if you have a program that can handle the relevant file type.

Windows knows which program to use for each type of file because it has a table that links each known file type to a program. This is the File Associations Table, and it is created automatically by Windows. If necessary, it can be edited manually. Manual intervention can be required when one program hijacks a common file type from another program.

Internet Explorer needs the aid of plug-in programs in order to handle some of the fancy graphics used on some web sites. These are mostly available as free downloads, and in some cases Windows can automatically download and install these plug-in programs.

When installing a program you will often be given various options that govern the way in which it is installed. The program should install properly and work well if you simply settle for all the default options. However, it is a good idea to read the notes that accompany each option, and to ensure that the installation program is not doing anything you would rather it did not do.

It is not essential to have any special software in order to download programs and other files. The built-in facilities of Windows do quite a good job, but there can be advantages in using a download manager. It is definitely a good idea to use one of these programs if you need to download large files using an ordinary dial-up connection.

Never take anything on the Internet at face value. You have to be especially careful when downloading and installing anything on your PC. What is supposed to be an innocent piece of software might actually be a virus, Trojan, or other type of malicious file. If in doubt, do not download it.

Install an antivirus program to help protect your PC against malicious files such as worms, viruses, and Trojans. Many new PCs are supplied with an antivirus program, and they can be obtained for nothing on the Internet. Windows XP has a built-in firewall program that will help to keep hackers at bay.

Having downloaded and installed a program it will often be necessary to go through some form of setting up process. This process should ensure that the program functions in a way that suits the user.

Index

Index

Index

Index

Index

Notes

Notes